Praise for *RRSPs*

"Gordon Pape is one of Canada's most influential writers about investing and personal finance. This plain-speaking, step-by-step guide to RRSPs helps readers set up a plan, understand how they work, and build successful strategies to make this all-important source of retirement income grow and prosper over time." —**Adam Mayers**, investment and personal-finance editor, *Toronto Star*

"Financial sage Gordon Pape pulls no punches: an RRSP is your personal pension plan and should be managed accordingly. Learn how to do just that in this easy-to-read book, which describes the journey to peace of mind in retirement." —**Evelyn Jacks**, bestselling author of 50 tax-planning books and president of Knowledge Bureau

"All you need to know about RRSPs from Canada's ultimate wealth expert." —**Rob Carrick**, personal-finance columnist, *The Globe and Mail*

"Gordon Pape has merged tax planning, hard truths, important information, and sage advice to create a comprehensive view of an RRSP: before, during, and after the set-up of the plan. Anyone who reads the book carefully will have learned everything he or she will likely need to know at any stage of the RRSP." —**Al Emid**

"Gordon Pape wants to banish the six words that can lead to financial ruin: 'I want to buy an RRSP.' After reading this book, you'll know how to make strategic investments in an RRSP (not purchases) and when to contribute to an RRSP compared to a tax-free savings account (TFSA). You'll find answers to all your questions here." —**Ellen Roseman**, personal-finance and consumer columnist, *Toronto Star*, and author of *Fight Back: 81 Ways to Help You Save Money and Protect Yourself from Corporate Trickery*

"Gordon Pape's latest guide to RRSPs provides all of the detailed information that readers of his previous guides have come to expect, as well as lots of useful advice on how investors can best make use of these invaluable tax-deferred retirement plans. If you only buy one financial guide this RRSP season, this should be the one." —**Gavin Graham**, chief strategy officer, INTEGRIS Pension Management

PORTFOLIO PENGUIN

RRSPs

GORDON PAPE is Canada's best-known financial author and the publisher of two investment newsletters: *The Income Investor* and the *Internet Wealth Builder*. He is the author/co-author of several national bestsellers, including *Tax-Free Savings Accounts*, *Retirement's Harsh New Realities*, *Money Savvy Kids*, and *Sleep-Easy Investing*. He has spoken at hundreds of seminars in Canada and the United States, is frequently quoted in the media, and is a popular guest on radio and television shows. His website is located at www.BuildingWealth.ca.

Also by Gordon Pape

INVESTMENT ADVICE

Tax-Free Savings Accounts
Money Savvy Kids
(with Deborah Kerbel)
Retirement's Harsh New Realities
The Ultimate TFSA Guide
Sleep-Easy Investing
The Retirement Time Bomb
Get Control of Your Money
6 Steps to $1 Million
Retiring Wealthy in the 21st Century
The Complete Guide to RRIFs and LIFs
(with David Tafler)
Gordon Pape's 2004 Buyer's Guide to
Mutual Funds (with Eric Kirzner)
Gordon Pape's 2004 Buyer's Guide
to RRSPs

Secrets of Successful Investing
(with Eric Kirzner)
Gordon Pape's Investing Strategies 2001
(with Richard Croft and Eric Kirzner)
Making Money in Mutual Funds
The Canadian Mortgage Book
(with Bruce McDougall)
The Best of Pape's Notes
Head Start (with Frank Jones)
Retiring Wealthy
Building Wealth in the '90s
Low-Risk Investing in the '90s
Low-Risk Investing
Building Wealth

CONSUMER ADVICE

Gordon Pape's International Shopping Advice (with Deborah Kerbel)

HUMOUR

The $50,000 Stove Handle

CHRISTMAS (with Deborah Kerbel)

Quizmas Carols
Family Quizmas
Quizmas: Christmas Trivia Family Fun

FICTION (with Tony Aspler)

Chain Reaction
The Scorpion Sanction
The Music Wars

NON-FICTION

Montreal at the Crossroads (with Donna Gabeline and Dane Lanken)

RRSPs

The Ultimate Wealth Builder

Gordon Pape

PORTFOLIO
PENGUIN

PORTFOLIO PENGUIN
an imprint of Penguin Canada Books Inc., a Penguin Random House Company

Published by the Penguin Group
Penguin Canada Books Inc., 90 Eglinton Avenue East, Suite 700, Toronto, Ontario, Canada M4P 2Y3

Penguin Group (USA) Inc., 375 Hudson Street, New York, New York 10014, U.S.A.
Penguin Books Ltd, 80 Strand, London WC2R 0RL, England
Penguin Ireland, 25 St Stephen's Green, Dublin 2, Ireland (a division of Penguin Books Ltd)
Penguin Group (Australia), 707 Collins Street, Melbourne, Victoria 3008, Australia
 (a division of Pearson Australia Group Pty Ltd)
Penguin Books India Pvt Ltd, 11 Community Centre, Panchsheel Park, New Delhi—110 017, India
Penguin Group (NZ), 67 Apollo Drive, Rosedale, Auckland 0632, New Zealand
 (a division of Pearson New Zealand Ltd)
Penguin Books (South Africa) (Pty) Ltd, 24 Sturdee Avenue, Rosebank, Johannesburg 2196,
 South Africa

Penguin Books Ltd, Registered Offices: 80 Strand, London WC2R 0RL, England

First published 2014

1 2 3 4 5 6 7 8 9 10 (WEB)

Copyright © Gordon Pape Enterprises Ltd., 2014

Manufactured in Canada.

LIBRARY AND ARCHIVES CANADA CATALOGUING IN PUBLICATION

Pape, Gordon, 1936–, author
RRSPs : the ultimate wealth builder / Gordon Pape.

Includes index.
ISBN 978-0-14-318921-3 (pbk.)

1. Registered Retirement Savings Plans. 2. Retirement income—Canada—Planning.
3. Saving and investment—Canada. I. Title.

HG179.P3755 2014   332.024'0145   C2013-907126-1

Visit the Penguin Canada website at **www.penguin.ca**

Special and corporate bulk purchase rates available; please see
www.penguin.ca/corporatesales or call 1-800-810-3104, ext. 2477.

To the memory of my beloved wife, Shirley Ann Pape.
I miss you.

Contents

1
A Look Back

Registered Retirement Savings Plans (RRSPs) have been around longer than most of today's Canadians. Pushing through the legislation creating them was one of the final acts of the Liberal government of Louis St. Laurent back in 1957. But the Liberals were gone from office, replaced by the Progressive Conservative government of John Diefenbaker, by the time the plans were officially launched the following year.

Giving Canadians a tax incentive to save for their own retirement was considered a radical idea at the time, but it made a lot of sense. The Canada and Quebec pension plans were still a decade down the road. The only income support for retirees without a workplace pension plan was Old Age Security. Clearly, something more was needed.

Few people realized the importance of the plan at the time. In fact, it was not even the centrepiece of the March budget introduced by the finance minister of the day, Walter Harris. With the Liberals knowing they were in trouble in the upcoming election, his focus was on the removal of an unpopular 10 percent tax on candy, gum, and soft drinks. Predictably, that's what grabbed the headlines. The RRSP news was relegated to page two.

The candy tax story has long since faded into oblivion. But RRSPs are still around all these years later and are arguably even more important today with the steady decline in the number of employees who have a workplace pension plan.

Of course, there have been many tweaks to the system over time, some good, some questionable. Among those in the "good" category, the steady increase in contribution room ranks at the top of the list. When RRSPs were launched, the most people were allowed to contribute each year was 10 percent of earned income to a maximum of $2500. By 2014, the limit had increased to 18 percent of the previous year's earned income to a maximum of $24,270.

Another huge improvement was the decision to allow unlimited carry-forwards for unused contribution room. Prior to 1991, it was a case of use it or lose it. If you didn't have the money to make a contribution in any given year, too bad. It was gone forever. That finally changed in 1991, but there was a time limit of seven years for making up unused contributions. That restriction was removed by Liberal finance minister Paul Martin in his 1996 budget, and since then unlimited carry-forwards have been permitted.

Originally, people could contribute to RRSPs until age 71. That changed in 1997 when the age limit was reduced to 69 as part of the federal government's austerity program to eliminate the high deficit that was threatening the country's credit rating. The Conservatives restored it to age 71 in the 2007 budget; now there is growing demand to have it bumped up again, with 73 being the age most often mentioned. The rationale is that since people are living longer, they should be allowed more time to save.

In the 1970s, Registered Retirement Income Funds (RRIFs) were added to the program. These were seen as the natural partners to RRSPs—the latter would be used for savings with the money moved into a RRIF in later years to provide a steady income stream. Prior to the creation of RRIFs, the only income option available for maturing RRSPs was the purchase of a life annuity—something many people were unwilling to do because it meant surrendering control of their money.

This is where the first of the questionable decisions comes into play. Originally, a RRIF had to be collapsed at age 90 with any remaining money withdrawn and taxed. That created a serious problem for people who had relied on RRIF income for a significant portion of their retirement cash flow. The federal government, after much lobbying, changed the rule in the 1992 budget, removing all age restrictions on RRIFs. But it did so at a price. All RRIFs set up after 1992 would have much higher minimum annual withdrawal rates. For example, a 71-year-old who opened a RRIF before 1993 would only have to take out 5.26 percent of the plan's value. Someone else of the same age whose plan was launched in 1993 or later had a minimum withdrawal requirement of 7.38 percent—more than two percentage points higher.

At the time, this didn't seem overly onerous, as interest rates were quite high. But by the second decade of the 21st century, RRIF holders were pleading for relief. A prolonged period of low interest rates meant that the plans were being drained of capital at an uncomfortably fast rate. Despite numerous entreaties, successive federal governments have done nothing up to now.

Another questionable decision was the 1992 move by the Progressive Conservative government of the day to introduce the Home Buyers' Plan (HBP). The economy was mired in a recession and the housing market was in particularly bad shape, so the Canadian Real Estate Association pressed Ottawa to provide some relief. The finance minister at the time, Don Mazankowski, responded with what was supposed to be a temporary program that allowed people to borrow up to $20,000 interest-free from RRSPs for a home purchase. The plan worked wonderfully; thousands of people took advantage of it, helping to turn around the depressed housing market.

So popular was it that the politicians were unwilling to let it die: Two years later, a new Liberal government made the HBP permanent. Finance Minister Paul Martin announced in his budget that it would continue to be an RRSP option. However, he did make one important change: Henceforth, only first-time homebuyers could use the plan. The HBP is still in place today, with the loan limit now at $25,000.

Having established the precedent, Ottawa decided to give people yet another excuse to dip into their RRSP money. On January 1, 1999, the Lifelong Learning Plan (LLP) came into effect. It allows people to borrow a maximum of $20,000 from their RRSPs, again interest-free, for the purpose of continuing education.

On the face of it, both programs appear to be worthwhile. Owning a home is the dream of most Canadian families, and every study has shown that more education improves job prospects and results in higher incomes.

The problem is that diverting money away from the prime purpose of RRSPs—saving for retirement—can lead to potential financial hardship down the road. Even if the loan is repaid in full—you're allowed 15 years to do that—the ultimate cost to an RRSP in terms of lost investment income may be in the tens of thousands of dollars. That's why I advise people to think very carefully and review all their options before tapping into either plan.

The RRSP story is still being written, so here are some of the changes I would like to see from future governments.

Raise the age limit. The age limit of 71 for having an RRSP is rapidly becoming outdated. The only reason it exists is so the government can force people to make taxable RRIF withdrawals even if they don't need the money. With the population aging and people living longer, the forced conversion to a RRIF or annuity at any time is becoming less defensible. Let each person decide when to tap into retirement savings and how much to take out. Eventually, whatever RRSP moneys remain will be taxed at death anyway.

Abolish the Home Buyers' Plan. The HBP may have met an economic need in the early 1990s but it has long since lost its raison d'être. In fact, the federal government has taken several steps in recent years to cool down what was seen as an overly heated housing market. Winding up the HBP would have been a good way to achieve that, but it appears to have never seriously been considered, perhaps because the government saw it as a vote-loser. Perhaps the program has become so embedded that no one dares attack it, but the reality is that it has become bad policy. The original reason for creating it no longer applies, and the inevitable result of using it is to reduce retirement assets.

2

Understanding the Lingo

The world of RRSPs has its own special language. Some of the words, terms, and acronyms may be new to you. So here is a glossary that you can refer to if something in this book puzzles you:

Accumulated income payments (AIPs). Unused amounts from Registered Education Savings Plans (RESP) that cannot be transferred to an RRSP and are therefore subject to a special tax.

Annuitant. The person who receives the retirement income created by an RRSP when the assets of the fund are invested in an annuity, a life income fund (LIF), a Registered Retirement Income Fund (RRIF), or a locked-in retirement income fund (LRIF). If the RRSP is in your name, you are the annuitant. If it is a spousal plan, your spouse is the annuitant.

Annuity. A regular income stream that is purchased from an insurance company using the capital in an RRSP or pension plan. Annuity payments may span a specific period, usually to age 90, or be in place for life.

Asset mix. The distribution of investments among different types of securities. Also known as asset allocation.

Assets. Any securities, deposits, or property that you own. In an RRSP, three basic types of assets may be held: cash, income, and growth.

Assets, cash. Securities or other property that can easily be converted to cash. Example: money market mutual funds.

Assets, growth. Securities or other property with the potential to produce capital gains. Examples: stocks, equity mutual funds.

Assets, income. Securities or other property that pays fixed rates of return. Example: guaranteed investment certificates (GICs).

Back-end load. A type of sales fee charged on mutual funds. A buyer pays no sales commission at the time of purchase but may be required to pay a redemption charge when the units are sold. This redemption fee, also known as a deferred sales charge, typically declines with the length of time that the fund is held by the investor.

Beneficiary. The person designated as heir to the assets of an RRSP in the event of the death of the annuitant. Married and common-law couples are advised to name their spouse/

partner or a dependent as the RRSP beneficiary, as this will permit a tax-free transfer of the money.

Bonds. Debt certificates issued by borrowers, usually governments or corporations, in order to raise capital for their business activities. Most bonds have a fixed interest rate and a set maturity date, at which time the principal will be repaid in full. A typical bond will pay interest semi-annually.

Book value. The cost of an investment at the time of purchase. At any given time, this cost may differ from the investment's current price—its market value.

Broker. A person who acts as an intermediary in the purchase of securities or insurance. For purposes of this book, the term "broker" will normally refer to a stockbroker unless otherwise indicated.

Call option. The right to purchase stock at a pre-determined price for a fixed period of time. A covered call is one in which the option seller actually owns the underlying stock. Call options are permitted in an RRSP.

Canada Premium Bonds (CPBs). Securities issued by the federal government. They were originally designed for retirement plans and education savings plans. The first series was issued for the 1997 RRSP season, and featured escalating interest rates over the 10-year life of the bond. Over time, however, the term has been reduced to three years and interest rates have fallen so low that few people use them any more.

Canada RRSP. A no-fee RRSP sponsored by the federal government, used to hold CPBs and Canada Savings Bonds (CSBs). Only existing plan holders can make contributions; no new plans are being opened.

Canada Savings Bonds (CSBs). Interest-bearing certificates issued by the Canadian government. Technically, these are not bonds, but a form of savings certificate. They are considered very safe investments because they can be cashed any time for their face value plus, if held for at least three months, any accrued interest. They were once very popular, but sales have now been restricted to payroll savings plans and interest rates are very low.

Capital gain/loss. The profit or loss made on the sale of an asset, calculated by subtracting the purchase price plus commissions from the sale price. Example: The capital gain on a stock purchased for $2000 and sold for $3000 with $100 in commissions is $900 ($3000 − $2100).

Carry-forward. The difference between a person's maximum allowable RRSP contribution and the amount of his or her actual contribution. Unused contribution entitlements accumulated after 1990 may be carried forward indefinitely.

Cashable GICs. Securities issued by a financial institution that bear interest at a fixed rate for a set period. Unlike regular guaranteed investment certificates (GICs), they can be cashed at any time after a holding period; however, a penalty will sometimes apply. Also called redeemable GICs.

Commuted annuity. An annuity that has been cashed in for a lump-sum payment.

Compounding. Growth of an investment and its accumulating profits over time. Compound growth rests on the concept of putting an ever-increasing amount of money to work, and can have a powerful effect on your savings rate.

Contribution deadline. The last date you can make an RRSP payment and earn a tax deduction for the previous year. It is 60 days after the end of the calendar year, so March 1, except in leap years.

Contribution in kind. An RRSP contribution in the form of a security, as opposed to cash.

Contribution limit. The maximum amount you can add to an RRSP in any year.

Contributor. A person who puts money into an RRSP.

Convertibles. Interest-bearing securities that may be exchanged for shares in a company at the request of the investor. Usually issued as bonds or preferred shares.

Coupons. Certificates that used to be attached to a bond, representing the interest payable by the bond issuer. Physical bond certificates are rarely issued any more; the whole process is done electronically. However, the rate of interest payable is still referred to as the "coupon rate."

Coupons, strip. Interest payments that have been removed from a bond's principal, also known as the "bond residue," and sold separately at a discounted price.

Creditor-proof. The term used to describe an RRSP that is protected from seizure by creditors in the event of personal bankruptcy or debt default. Insurance company RRSPs are usually creditor-proof, but there are circumstances under which they have no such protection.

Deferred profit-sharing plan (DPSP). A plan in which business profits are shared with employees. Such a plan must be registered with the Canada Revenue Agency (CRA) in order to qualify for tax benefits.

Deferred sales charge. A fee charged when units of a mutual fund purchased with a back-end load option are redeemed. (See also: back-end load.)

Deposit insurance. Coverage of certain types of assets against financial failure. Banks and most trust and loan companies are members of the Canada Deposit Insurance Corporation (CDIC). Credit unions are covered by provincial agencies.

Derivatives. Contracts that allow holders to buy or sell specific securities at a future date, at a specified price. Most derivative contracts trade on a stock market.

Distributions. Periodic payments made by mutual funds, exchange-traded funds (ETFs), real estate investment trusts (REITs), etc.

Diversification. An investment technique intended to minimize risk by placing money in a number of securities with different risk/return characteristics.

Dividend tax credit. A special tax credit intended to reduce the effective rate of tax paid by investors on dividend income. The rationale is that Canadian corporations have already paid tax on their earnings and are distributing dividends out of this after-tax income.

Dividends. Payments made to shareholders of a company or a mutual fund. These may be in the form of cash or additional shares or units.

Dollar-cost averaging. The practice of investing a fixed amount of money in a security on a regular basis over a period of time. The goal is to smooth out variations in the purchase prices.

Earned income. For RRSP purposes, the eligible income that is used to calculate an individual's maximum contribution limit. Generally, earned income includes income from employment but excludes income from investments or pensions.

Exchange-traded fund (ETF). A fund that trades on a stock exchange. Most ETFs represent shares of ownership in vehicles that hold portfolios of common stocks designed to correspond to the price and performance of underlying portfolios of securities. They usually track a specific equity index or sub-index (e.g., gold, energy, REITs), but there are several that are bond-based.

Financial adviser. A person who assists investors in their decision-making. This may be a broker, mutual fund sales representative, bank staffer, or financial planner.

Foreign property. Securities that are issued by non-Canadian companies or governments. There used to be a limit on the percentage of foreign property allowed in an RRSP, but this has been eliminated.

Front-end load. A sales commission charged at the time of purchase of units of a mutual fund.

Group RRSP. A plan set up by an employer for the staff. The employer cannot make direct contributions to the plan, but employees benefit from lower costs.

Guaranteed investment certificates (GICs). Securities issued by financial institutions, such as banks and trust companies. A typical GIC bears a fixed rate of interest and cannot be cashed before maturity. GICs with terms of up to five years issued by members of the CDIC are covered by deposit insurance to a maximum of $100,000. GICs issued by credit unions are protected by provincial insurance plans and coverage varies from one province to another. GICs are traditionally popular in RRSPs because of the security they provide. However, in recent years returns have been low.

Home Buyers' Plan (HBP). A program that allows first-time homebuyers to borrow up to $25,000 from RRSP savings interest-free to purchase a residential property. There is a set payback schedule for such loans.

iShares. The dominant ETF brand in this country, owned by BlackRock Canada.

Income trusts. A security that holds cash-generating assets in the form of a trust, paying out the profits directly to investors. At one time they were very popular, but a special tax that took effect in 2011 forced most income trusts to convert to corporations.

Index. A measure of how a particular market is performing based on the performance of selected stocks or bonds. An index serves as a benchmark by which to measure the performance of a particular investment.

Interest. The income investors receive in return for giving an institution the use of their money. On bonds and bank accounts, this is expressed as an annual or a daily percentage.

Interest, accrued. The amount of interest owed on a loan at a given time.

Interest, compound. Interest paid on the original principal plus any reinvested interest.

Investment. A security purchased for income or profit. Examples: stocks, bonds, ETFs, and mutual funds.

Investment, aggressive. A security with a high degree of risk. The potential return on aggressive investments is above average but so is the possibility of loss. Example: equity mutual funds.

Investment, conservative. A security not prone to large losses but with relatively low growth potential. These types of investments may be especially well suited to RRSPs and other plans in which low risk is desirable. Example: guaranteed investment certificates.

Investment, speculative. A security with an extremely high level of risk and little or no established record of profit. Speculative investments may result in heavy losses, so they are not suitable for most RRSPs. Example: penny mining stocks.

Investment income. Payments received from securities, usually in the form of interest or dividends.

Life Income Fund (LIF). A retirement income option for those with locked-in RRSPs. Investments held in a LIF are subject to government-regulated annual minimum and maximum payouts. It used to be that some provinces required the assets of a LIF to be converted to a life annuity at age 80; however, this has been eliminated in most cases.

Lifelong Learning Plan (LLP). A program that allows you to borrow up to $20,000 from an RRSP interest-free for post-secondary education.

Liquidity. The quality of a security that allows it to be converted easily to cash.

Load. The commission charged when mutual fund units are bought (front-end load) or sold (back-end load).

Locked-in Retirement Account (LIRA). See: locked-in RRSP.

Locked-in Retirement Income Fund (LRIF). A locked-in plan that offers more flexibility than a LIF. Not available in all provinces.

Locked-in RRSP. An RRSP in which assets originate from a pension plan. In the past, the assets could only be accessed by the plan holder after retirement. However, the federal government and many provinces now allow earlier withdrawals under certain conditions. At maturity, locked-in RRSPs can be converted to LIFs, LRIFs where available, or life annuities. Also known as a Locked-in Retirement Account (LIRA).

Management fees. Charges made to a mutual fund by its managers in compensation for services. These payments are drawn from the assets of the fund. In general, the size of the management fee has a significant effect on overall fund performance; the greater the portion of assets paid to the manager, the lower the fund's return.

Marginal tax rate. The tax rate payable on the last dollar you earn. In an RRSP your savings are sheltered from tax until the money is withdrawn.

Maximum amount. The largest amount you can withdraw from a LIF in any year. The limits are set by provincial governments except for LIFs that fall under federal jurisdiction.

Meltdown. A strategy for withdrawing RRSP funds early so as to reduce the tax hit when the plan holder dies.

Minimum amount. The smallest amount you're required to withdraw from a RRIF/LIF in any given year. Annual minimums are regulated by the federal government and are set as a percentage of total RRIF/LIF assets. No withdrawals are required during the year the plan is created.

Mutual funds. Pools of investment money managed by professionals. Mutual funds may invest in a wide range of securities, from stocks to mortgages.

Mutual funds, balanced. Funds that hold a mixture of stocks, bonds, and cash.

Mutual funds, bond. Funds that concentrate their assets in fixed-income securities such as government and/or corporate bonds. Since bond funds tend to be actively managed, they do not offer the predictable yield that an investor would get from buying high-quality bonds.

Mutual funds, closed-end. Funds in which the total number of shares issued is limited. These resemble stocks in that, if shares are not purchased at the initial offering, they must be purchased from an existing owner, usually via a stock exchange.

Mutual funds, equity. Funds that invest in stocks.

Mutual funds, fixed-income. Funds that invest in securities, such as bonds and mortgages, that pay interest at a fixed rate.

Mutual funds, high-yield. Funds that invest in securities that generate above-average income streams. Typical holdings of high-yield funds include stocks with above-average dividends, real estate investment trusts, limited partnerships, and low-grade (junk) bonds.

Mutual funds, load. Funds that allow sales representatives or brokers to charge a commission when units are bought or sold.

Mutual funds, money market. Funds that invest in short-term securities, such as treasury bills. These funds offer investors an inexpensive way to hold cash reserves but returns are minimal in times of low interest rates.

Mutual funds, mortgage. Funds that invest primarily in residential first mortgages.

Mutual funds, no-load. Funds that have no obvious sales commission or redemption charges. These funds still have management and operating costs that are charged to the investor.

Mutual funds, open-end. Funds that place no limit on the number of units issued. New units are offered continuously and are purchased directly from the fund's treasury.

Mutual funds, precious metals. Funds that invest in precious metals, mainly gold, but including silver and palladium. A fund may invest in the metal itself, shares in mining companies, or a combination of both.

Mutual funds, real estate. Funds that invest in real estate, usually commercial and industrial. Although a few of these funds hold real property directly, because of concerns about liquidity, most choose to invest in the shares of companies that participate in the sector such as developers, property managers, and financiers.

Net asset value (NAV). The value of a mutual fund unit at any given time. It is calculated by subtracting the fund's liabilities from its assets and dividing by the number of units outstanding. Open-end mutual funds are bought and sold at their net asset value.

Non-registered investments. Savings kept outside an RRSP, RRIF, Tax-Free Savings Account (TFSA), etc.

Overcontribution. An amount contributed to an RRSP in excess of your permitted entitlement. Also called excess contributions. The overcontribution room is intended to forgive inadvertent miscalculations on the part of individuals, though it may be used as a deliberate strategy. You may overcontribute a cumulative total of $2000 to an RRSP without penalty, after which you'll be charged 1 percent a month on the overage. No immediate tax deduction may be claimed in respect to overcontributions, but you may draw on the money for future deductions.

Past service pension adjustment (PSPA). Adjustments made to your pension plan that allow you to upgrade benefits or retroactively add periods of pensionable service.

Penalties. Special assessments by the CRA for violating RRSP rules. These usually take the form of a special tax of 1 percent a month.

Pension adjustment (PA). A calculation of the value of contributions made on your behalf to an employer-sponsored pension plan or DPSP during a given year. The calculation takes into account the amounts contributed by employer and employee as well as the retirement benefits that will eventually accrue. The PA affects the RRSP contribution room of a pension plan member.

Pension adjustment reversal (PAR). A recalculation of previous pension adjustments in the event an individual will not be entitled to full benefits, usually because of early termination. The effect of a PAR is to restore lost RRSP contribution room.

Pension plan, defined benefit. A plan in which pension payments are guaranteed on the basis of a set formula. Example: Payments are based on the average of the best three years of earnings multiplied by 2 percent times the number of years of service. If the best three years averaged $60,000, an employee with 30 years of service would draw an annual pension of $36,000 ($60,000 × .02 × 30).

Pension plan, defined contribution. A plan in which there is no guarantee of the amount to be paid. The pension is determined by total contributions and the returns earned by the invested money. Also known as money purchase plans.

Pooled Registered Pension Plans (PRPPs). A program approved by Ottawa in 2012 that allows small businesses and self-employed people to participate in a privately managed pension fund. Provincial ratification is required before the plans can be launched.

Portfolio. All the investments held by a person. If the investments are held in an RRSP, the portfolio is considered to be "registered," and any growth is not subject to tax until money is withdrawn.

Put option. The right to sell a stock at a pre-determined price for a fixed period of time. Put options are not permitted in RRSPs.

Qualified beneficiary. A person who is entitled to receive the proceeds of an RRSP tax-free. In most cases this will be a surviving spouse.

Qualified investment. A security or other investment deemed by the federal government to be eligible for inclusion in an RRSP. Non-qualified investments (undeveloped land is one example) may not be included in a registered retirement plan. Also called eligible investments.

Real estate investment trusts (REITs). Trusts that specialize in real estate investments. They trade on stock exchanges and have become popular with RRSP investors in recent years, although the tax advantages they offer are lost in a registered plan.

Refund of premiums. Amounts paid from an RRSP on the death of the plan holder to the annuitant's spouse. A dependent child or grandchild may also qualify for a refund of premium payments.

Registered Education Savings Plan (RESP). A government-approved program that offers help in saving for a child's future education. Although RESP contributions do not generate tax refunds, earnings within a plan grow tax-free. RESP earnings may be transferred into an RRSP, with certain conditions, if the intended beneficiary does not go on to post-secondary education.

Registered Pension Plan (RPP). A pension plan registered with the CRA in order to obtain tax relief for contributions.

Registered Retirement Income Fund (RRIF). A government-registered retirement fund set up with proceeds from an RRSP. A minimum amount must be withdrawn annually, in accordance with a set formula. Contributions to a RRIF are not permitted, although transfers from other registered plans are allowed under certain circumstances.

Registered Retirement Savings Plan (RRSP). A program designed to encourage Canadians to save for retirement by providing tax deductions for contributions and tax-sheltered growth for earnings inside the plan. All RRSPs must be registered with the CRA.

Retail venture capital funds. Mutual funds that benefit from special tax treatment by the federal government and from some provincial governments. The goal is to provide seed capital to fledgling companies; investors get tax breaks for supporting such start-ups. They are high-risk in nature and may be headed for extinction since the federal government's 2013 budget announced phasing out of its tax credit. Also known as labour-sponsored funds.

Retiring allowance. A lump-sum payment received on termination of employment. A portion of a retiring allowance may be eligible for direct transfer to an RRSP.

Return. The amount of money earned by an investment. The rate of return is the percentage this represents. Example: A $1000 investment that produced a return of $50 over 12 months would have an annual rate of return of 5 percent.

Risk. The extent to which an investment is exposed to potential losses. A loss can take several forms, ranging from a decline in value in relation to the original purchase price to an erosion in purchasing power due to inflation. There are no investments that are completely risk-free, but some, such as Government of Canada treasury bills, come close.

Segregated funds. Similar to mutual funds, but sold as part of insurance contracts. They offer certain benefits not available with regular mutual funds, such as guarantees of principal on maturity and death benefits.

Self-directed RRSP. A plan in which the individual makes all the investment decisions. Also called a self-administered plan.

Spousal RRSP. A plan in which contributions are made by one spouse for the benefit of another (including a common-law spouse or partner). The ultimate goal is to split income in retirement. Contributions and withdrawals from a spousal plan are subject to special rules laid down by the CRA.

Spouse. For RRSP purposes, a person to whom you are legally married or living with in a common-law relationship, including same-sex couples.

Stock market. An organization that facilitates the buying and selling of shares in public companies. The Toronto Stock Exchange (TSX) is the largest one in Canada.

Stock market, bear. The term used to describe a market in which the general value of shares is falling.

Stock market, bull. The term used to describe a market in which the general value of shares is rising.

Stock market index. A measure of a market's performance and, indirectly, of the economy. The S&P/TSX Composite Index is based on approximately 300 leading stocks listed on the Toronto Stock Exchange, and is the most widely quoted in Canada.

Stocks. Shares in public companies, representing ownership or "equity." They may or may not trade on recognized stock exchanges. Common stocks usually (but not always) carry voting rights. Preferred stocks usually do not have voting rights but often pay a higher dividend.

Stocks, blue-chip. A term used to describe shares in sound, well-established companies, usually with a long history of consistent dividend payments.

Stocks, concept. Shares in small companies that may have a good business idea but no significant production or sales on record.

Stocks, growth. Shares that have strong potential to appreciate in value.

Stocks, penny. Shares in junior companies that usually trade for less than a dollar each. Most Canadian stocks of this type trade on the Toronto Venture Exchange. Such stocks are considered highly speculative and generally are not recommended for RRSPs.

Stocks, unlisted. Shares that do not trade on a recognized stock exchange.

Strip bonds. Bonds from which interest coupons have been removed, or "stripped." They are sold at a discount and redeemed for face value at maturity. The difference between the purchase price and face value represents the bond holder's return. Also called zero-coupon bonds.

Swap. Exchanging a security outside an RRSP for one already in the plan.

Switching. Moving money from one mutual fund to another. Many mutual fund companies allow switching among their own funds with little or no charge.

Taxable income. The amount of income subject to tax after all possible deductions have been claimed.

Tax-Free Savings Account (TFSA). A tax-sheltered savings/investment plan. It differs from RRSPs in that there is no tax deduction for a contribution. However, when money is withdrawn, it comes out tax-exempt.

Term deposit (TD). A security issued by a financial institution that bears a fixed rate of interest. Basically the same as GICs, the difference is that term deposits usually mature in less than a year. Some term deposits may be cashed before maturity, usually with a penalty.

Treasury bills (T-bills). Short-term securities issued by governments and sold at retail by stockbrokers and banks. Those issued by the Government of Canada are regarded as excellent short-term investments because of their safety and competitive returns.

Unit. A share in a mutual fund.

Unused contribution room. The difference between your annual RRSP deduction limit and the amount you actually contribute. Example: If your deduction limit for the current year is $15,000 and you contribute $8000, your unused contribution room is $7000.

Vested benefits. Benefits earned from a Registered Pension Plan or DPSP to which you remain entitled even if you leave the company.

Withholding tax. Tax deducted at source on foreign dividends. U.S. dividends paid into an RRSP are exempt, but those paid by a company domiciled elsewhere may not be.

3
The Rules of the Game

At first glance, RRSPs seem to be very straightforward. You put money into a plan, get your tax refund, and move on. If only life were that simple! The reality is that the many rules and regulations governing RRSPs amount to a bureaucratic labyrinth. Even professionals sometimes have difficulty interpreting some of the more arcane points, so don't be dismayed if you find yourself scratching your head on whether a certain investment is qualified or if you are eligible for the HBP.

Here is a rundown of some of the most important rules that you need to know. You'll find more detailed explanations in the relevant chapters later in the book.

Carry-forwards. You may carry forward unused deduction entitlements indefinitely. For example, if you were allowed to contribute $5000 last year but only had $2000 available to invest, the unused $3000 can be used this year or any time in the future.

Contribution limit. The amount you can legally contribute to your RRSP for any given year is 18 percent of the previous year's earned income, to a maximum allowable amount. To illustrate, suppose you had earned income of $60,000 in 2013. The maximum you can contribute for the 2014 tax year is $10,800 ($60,000 × .18). High-income earners are capped at a maximum of $23,820 for 2013, increasing to $24,270 in 2014. The maximum amount is indexed, so will change annually. Members of RPPs and DPSPs will have their contribution limit reduced by their pension adjustment (PA).

Contributions in kind. You may contribute securities such as stocks, bonds, mutual funds, GICs, and ETFs directly to a self-directed RRSP. However, for tax purposes the securities will be deemed to have been sold on the day of the contribution. Any capital gain at that point will be taxable. However, unfair as it may seem, you are not allowed to claim a capital loss if you contribute a money-losing security. In that case, you should sell the security first, thereby triggering an allowable capital loss, and then contribute the cash proceeds to the RRSP.

Deadline. The last day for contributions to be eligible for deduction in the previous tax year is 60 days after year-end. In most years, that date will be March 1; in leap years, the date is February 29.

Death. Any money in your RRSPs will be included in your income in the year of your death and taxed accordingly. You can avoid this tax bite by making your spouse or a dependent child or grandchild the beneficiary of your plan. He or she can then transfer all the money directly into his/her RRSP and defer the tax. You can designate your spouse or a dependent offspring as beneficiary when you complete the forms to set up an RRSP. That way, the funds will go directly to him/her if anything happens to you, without the time and expense of probate. If your estate is currently the designated beneficiary of your RRSP, make arrangements to switch to your spouse or a dependent offspring. The financial institution that holds your plan can provide the required forms. If you have not yet designated a beneficiary, make a point of doing so soon.

Deductibility. The full amount of your allowable RRSP contribution may be deducted from your taxable income in order to lower your tax liability. However, you don't have to claim the deduction in the year you make a contribution if it is beneficial to defer it to a later date. For example, if you expect to be in a higher tax bracket next year (perhaps because you are only working part-time now), it could work to your advantage to postpone claiming the deduction until that time. Remember, the higher your marginal tax rate, the more money an RRSP deduction will save. This makes it more valuable than a tax credit for higher-income people.

Earned income. This often causes confusion. It includes income earned from any type of employment as well as money received from taxable support payments, disability payments from the Canada or Quebec pension plans, and net rental income. Pension income and investment profits other than rental income don't qualify. The CRA has a form for calculating earned income in its guide titled *RRSPs and Other Registered Plans for Retirement.*

Eligibility. Everyone who is age 71 or younger may contribute to an RRSP, as long as they have earned income in the previous year or carry-forward room. If you are older than 71 but have a younger spouse, you may contribute to a spousal RRSP on his/her behalf, again if you have earned income. There is no minimum age for setting up an RRSP. Even an infant can have a plan, as long as he or she has earned income (for instance, from appearing in a television commercial).

Home purchase loans. You may borrow up to $25,000 from your RRSP interest-free for the purchase of a qualified home under the HBP.

Interest expense. Interest incurred on loans in order to contribute to an RRSP is not tax deductible.

Lifelong Learning Plan. This program allows you to borrow up to $20,000 from your RRSP interest-free for purposes of continuing your education. Any missed repayments will be added to your income and taxed.

Number of plans. You can open as many separate RRSPs with as many financial institutions as you like; there is no limit. However, while multiple RRSPs allow you greater flexibility, they can also create problems. Too many plans may be difficult to manage. Also, they can be expensive, depending on what types of RRSPs you set up. A typical self-directed plan will have an annual administration fee of $100 or more plus assorted other costs, such as transaction fees for certain types of trades. So even though there's no official limit, common sense should prevail. Often, it's better to consolidate several plans into one self-directed RRSP for ease of administration and reduced cost.

Overcontributions. You're allowed to make overcontributions to your plan without penalty as long as you are age 19 or older and they don't exceed a total of $2000 at any time. Amounts in excess of $2000 are subject to a penalty tax of 1 percent monthly. You may use overcontributions for future RRSP deductions, as long as you have earned income in the given year. You're allowed to withdraw overcontributions, but if you do so before they're certified by the CRA on form T3012A, the amount withdrawn will be subject to withholding tax. If you pay tax, you can reclaim it when you file your next return.

Pension income. You may not roll any periodic pension income directly into your personal RRSP. However, lump-sum payments from a pension plan may be rolled over.

Prohibited investments. A few types of investments may not be held in an RRSP. They include real estate, a loan to yourself, shares or debt in a company in which you have a "significant interest" (usually more than 10 percent ownership), and any debt or shares in a corporation with which you do not deal at arm's length.

Qualified investments. A wide range of investments is allowed in an RRSP, including GICs, term deposits, treasury bills, Canada Savings and Canada Premium bonds, savings certificates, Government of Canada bonds, provincial government bonds, Crown corporation bonds, bonds issued by Canadian corporations listed on a recognized stock exchange, strip bonds, foreign government investment-grade bonds, Canadian stocks listed on recognized exchanges, shares of foreign companies listed on recognized exchanges and bonds issued by such foreign companies, American Depositary Receipts (ADRs), some limited partnership units, some U.S. and Canadian over-the-counter stocks, shares of small businesses (under certain conditions), mutual funds, ETFs, mortgages (including your own), call options, warrants and rights issued by companies listed on Canadian exchanges, bankers' acceptances, and Canadian cash. As a result of changes made in 2005, you can now also own gold and silver in a variety of forms: investment-grade coins, bars, ingots, wafers, ETFs, and mutual funds. In short, most types of securities are eligible. Surprisingly, however, there is no official list available that clearly states which investments qualify. As of spring 2013, officials of the CRA were reworking IT Bulletin 320, the generally used resource, which had not been updated since July 2002. However, a senior CRA official told me that even when completed, the bulletin still will not include a comprehensive list of qualified investments "but will include references to some of the changes to the qualified investments rules since 2002." My reply was that I found this surprising. Tax law compliance requires as much clarity as possible so that people can understand the laws and regulations. It is the government's responsibility to make this information readily available; failure to do so is inexcusable.

Receipts. When you make an RRSP contribution, you'll be issued an official tax receipt by the institution that administers the plan. You must file this receipt with your tax return in order to claim an RRSP deduction. If you've lost it, ask the financial institution to issue a duplicate.

Registration. All RRSPs must be officially registered with the CRA to qualify for tax deductions and other special tax treatment. Your financial institution will look after this.

Retiring allowances. Special payments received as a result of employment termination may be rolled directly into an RRSP. These payments include rewards for long service, unused sick-leave credits, and compensation for being fired. The amount you're allowed to transfer directly to your RRSP is $2000 times the number of years, or part years, you worked for the employer, up to and including 1995. No credit is given for subsequent years; however, if you have available RRSP room, you may use it for this purpose. In addition, if you have no vested pension or DPSP benefits, you're allowed an additional $1500 for each year you were with the employer prior to 1989.

Spousal plans. You may set up an RRSP for your spouse and contribute to it as long as he or she is age 71 or younger. The total contributions you make to your own plan plus the spousal plan must be within your personal limit. Note that common-law and same-sex couples are also allowed to create spousal plans. There are restrictions on when withdrawals can be made from these plans.

Swaps. You may not exchange or "swap" a security in your RRSP for one outside the plan, even if they are of comparable value. This is due to a rule change announced in the 2011 budget. At that time, swaps were deemed to be "advantages." The penalty for violation is a confiscatory 100 percent of the amount involved. At the time, the CRA issued a fact sheet that stated: "These rules strongly discourage individuals from undertaking any swap transaction with their registered plan by eliminating all current and future benefits associated with the transaction."

Transfers. If you have more than one RRSP, you are allowed to move assets from one RRSP to another without penalty. Simply complete form T2033, which is available on the CRA website. Alternatively, your financial institution should be able to provide its own version of the transfer form or execute the transfer electronically. Note that you cannot transfer RRSP assets into a TFSA.

Withdrawals. Any withdrawals from an RRSP are taxable at your marginal rate. You are allowed to withdraw part of the assets from a plan without de-registering the entire plan.

4
Get the Right Plan

There are lots of ways you can go off the track with an RRSP. But the most common mistake is the one many people make from the get-go: They walk into their local bank and say to the teller: "I want to buy an RRSP."

Those six words can lead to a world of financial hurt. Resolve never to utter them.

For starters, you don't "buy" an RRSP, any more than you would buy a savings account. You invest in one. Think of an RRSP as a large empty box into which you can put almost any type of security you wish—provided you select the right type of plan.

That brings us to the second error in the sentence. Never tell someone that you want to open an RRSP without first knowing exactly what type of plan you want. Vague statements will likely result in a savings account plan or one that can invest only in GICs, which may not be what you want at all.

The type of RRSP you select will have a huge impact on how your money will grow over the years, so make sure you get it right. Here are your options, with the advantages and disadvantages of each.

Savings RRSPs

This is the most basic type of plan. It is really nothing more than a tax-sheltered savings account. Some financial institutions offer special rates for this type of RRSP, but your money is not going to grow very quickly as long as interest rates are low.

Advantages. Your money is safe. If the account is with a federally chartered institution, such as a major bank, it will be protected by deposit insurance up to $100,000. Credit unions are covered by provincial insurance plans, which vary across the country.

A savings plan is also simple to understand and manage. You make your contribution, let it sit in the account, and collect interest periodically. That makes it a good fit for people who don't want to be bothered with complex investing decisions. If you can handle a bank account, you can manage a savings RRSP.

Disadvantages. You'll get a lousy return. Watching your money grow will be like watching a snail race—it will take a long time to get anywhere. When interest rates rise, your return will improve, but it will still be much less than you could expect to earn in another type of plan.

Conclusion. Savings plans are only suitable for ultra-conservative investors whose main concern is getting a tax refund and who don't care if the RRSP grows at a very slow pace.

GIC RRSPs

If a request for a generic RRSP doesn't result in a savings plan, this is what you're likely to end up with. Your money will be used to purchase a five-year GIC with a set rate of return. Every fifth year, on the anniversary date, the original GIC will be rolled over at the prevailing rate at the time unless you give instructions to the contrary. Usually, you will not be notified that the GIC is about to mature. The bank will just roll it over automatically.

Advantages. You'll earn a higher rate of return than you'll receive from a savings account although you won't get rich as long as rates remain low. Generally, the major banks offer much lower rates than smaller financial institutions. However, if you are a good customer, you may be able to negotiate an extra quarter-point or even a half-point. It doesn't hurt to ask.

GICs that mature in five years or less also offer the same level of safety as a savings plan, with deposit insurance coverage of up to $100,000 for member companies of the CDIC.

Other advantages include simplicity and consistency. Basic GICs are easy to understand and provide a predictable rate of return. However, avoid the more complex index-linked GICs, where the return is tied to the performance of a stock market index, a basket of shares or mutual funds, or some other measure. These GICs can be infuriatingly difficult to understand and are totally unpredictable in terms of what your eventual return might be.

Disadvantages. For starters, your money is locked in for the term of the certificate, typically five years. That's fine when interest rates appear poised to fall, but it's not a good idea when rates are low. Two or three years down the road you may find your money is earning much less than current rates are offering.

If you invest when rates are low, inflation becomes a potential problem. In recent years, cost-of-living increases have been low, but don't lose sight of the fact that the Bank of Canada aims for a 2-percent annual inflation rate. If we should get back to that and you have money in GICs that is earning only slightly more, your gain in terms of real purchasing power will be minimal.

Automatic rollovers are another negative. You should have the option to decide if you want to reinvest the money and, if so, for how long at each maturity date. Ask the RRSP provider to ensure you receive regular notification of maturing GICs.

Conclusion. GICs are suitable for very conservative investors but returns will be limited when interest rates are low. The best approach is to create a GIC ladder with some of your money rolling over each year for reinvestment. That way you'll be in a position to benefit when rates move up.

Mutual Fund RRSPs

As the name suggests, these plans invest in a portfolio of mutual funds. They are offered by all banks and most credit unions and are also available through brokers, mutual fund dealers, and, in some cases, directly from the fund companies themselves. Insurance companies offer a variation of these, using segregated funds—mutual funds with extras attached, such as loss protection.

Advantages. For starters, you are hiring a professional to look after your money in the person of the fund manager. Of course, that doesn't mean you'll automatically get rich—some fund managers have proven over time they are not much better than the crowd. But most managers will probably do better than you would if you had to make all the buy/sell decisions.

You also get instant diversification. Whatever type of fund you choose will contain a variety of securities, sometimes several hundred of them. If you select a balanced fund, you'll own a mix of stocks, bonds, and cash, perhaps with some international exposure as a bonus.

A carefully managed mutual fund plan has more growth potential than either a savings- or GIC-based RRSP. A conservative plan should be able to generate an average annual return of between 5 percent and 6 percent over time. One that is more aggressive (takes greater risks) could return 7 percent to 8 percent annually.

Disadvantages. You'll move to a higher level of risk—perhaps much higher, depending on the funds you select. Mutual funds are not covered by deposit insurance so you have no protection against loss (except in the case of segregated funds). And of course, the nature of the investments made by the fund manager carry risk, with equity funds especially vulnerable to stock market corrections. You can mitigate the risk by weighting your portfolio towards fixed-income and money market funds, but that will also reduce the return potential.

Costs are another concern. You may be charged a sales commission when you buy the funds, although that is becoming less common. If you purchase deferred sales charge (DSC) units, you'll be hit with a sales commission if you sell within a certain time, typically seven years.

On top of sales commissions, you'll pay an annual fee to own the funds. This is expressed as a management expense ratio (MER). It's the percentage of fees and expenses paid out by the fund as a portion of total assets. The average Canadian equity fund has an MER of around 2.5 percent. Many people don't realize that a large chunk of this money goes to paying an annual "trailer fee" to your financial adviser. This is usually 1 percent for an equity fund but could be as high as 1.5 percent. Fixed-income and money market funds pay lower trailers and thus usually have reduced MERs.

Your choice of funds may be limited, depending on who holds your plan. Some financial institutions offer only their own funds. Others include a range of third-party funds in their lineup. You'll find some brokers and dealers don't offer funds from companies that don't pay trailers, such as Calgary-based Mawer Investment Management and the Steadyhand Investment Funds of Vancouver.

Conclusion. Mutual funds are a quick and easy way to create a diversified portfolio, but they can be expensive and you must choose carefully. Look for a plan that offers a wide range of fund choices; don't tie yourself to a single company.

Multi-Purpose Plans

These plans offer a combination of the first three types we have looked at: savings, GICs, and mutual funds. Many banks and credit unions offer them, although you may have to ask if they are an option.

Advantages. You have much greater flexibility with these plans. You can invest in a combination of GICs, mutual funds, and cash depending on your view of economic conditions and your risk tolerance level.

The portion of your assets that is held in GICs and cash will be protected by deposit insurance so at least part of your RRSP will be insulated from financial disaster. This means you can more tightly control the risk element within the plan.

Disadvantages. Each component of these RRSPs comes with the same disadvantages I described earlier in this chapter. In addition, there may be a higher annual administration fee for these plans. Ask about costs before committing.

Conclusion. This is a better choice than any of the first three mentioned because of the greatly increased flexibility.

Self-Directed Plans

If you like the idea of calling all the shots in your RRSP, this is the plan for you. Available mainly through brokers, self-directed plans enable you to invest in every type of RRSP-eligible security: stocks, bonds, ETFs, mutual funds, GICs, gold, cash—you name it.

There are two variations of the self-directed plan. The most common model requires you to pay brokerage commissions on every stock trade and, in some cases, sales commissions on fund purchases. However, fee-based accounts are becoming more popular. With these plans, you pay an annual fee based on the assets in the RRSP—1.5 percent is typical. In return, you get free stock trades and commission-free mutual fund "F" units, which also carry a reduced MER.

Advantages. These plans provide the ultimate in flexibility. Almost every government-approved security can be held. I say "almost" because very few companies allow you to hold your own mortgage in an RRSP, even though it is legal to do so, due to the paperwork involved. Some companies also discourage shares in private companies, even though they too are legal, provided they meet certain conditions.

A well-managed self-directed plan offers much more growth potential than other types of RRSPs. A target of 8 percent annually over the long term is not unrealistic. These plans also encourage investors to learn more about the markets and to pay close attention to the performance of each security held.

Disadvantages. Risk is the number-one concern. Holders of self-directed plans tend to invest a high proportion of their assets in stocks and equity mutual funds, which can be volatile at times. Remember that an RRSP is really a personal pension plan, so preserving capital should always be a major factor in portfolio building.

Self-directed plans are also the most expensive type of RRSP to own. You'll usually be assessed an annual administration fee plus you'll have to pay commissions on each trade, unless you select a fee-based account. Keep an eye on the costs; they can chew into your RRSP's profits at an alarming rate.

The other factor to consider is the time commitment. It requires attention and discipline to successfully manage a self-directed RRSP. These plans should be carefully reviewed at least quarterly and preferably monthly. Ask yourself whether you are willing to devote that amount of time to looking after your plan. If the answer is no, choose another option.

Conclusion. Self-directed plans offer the most profit potential, but they come with more risk and are expensive and time-consuming to manage.

The Bottom Line

If you're just opening your first RRSP, you now have all the information you need to choose the type best suited for your needs. But what if you already have a plan, and after reading this, you've decided it's not really what you want? You have two options.

The first is to leave the old plan in place, at least for now, and open a new account where future contributions can be directed. This may be the best course if the financial institution that holds your current plan wants to charge you a high fee for closing and transferring. However, you may be able to move to a different type of plan within the same organization at no cost.

Your second option is to move all the assets into a brand new plan, having first ascertained the cost of doing so. Financial institutions used to take weeks to implement such transfers, but under pressure from regulators, they have speeded up the process.

Do not make the mistake of cashing out an existing plan with the idea of taking the money to another financial institution. That would result in a large tax bill because the amount withdrawn will be treated as income in the year it is received. Instead, open the new plan, and then arrange for a direct transfer from the old RRSP. That can be done tax-free. The financial institution that gets the new business will handle the paperwork for you.

5
Building a Winning RRSP

Let's get one thing clear from the start. RRSPs are not all about making a contribution and collecting a juicy tax refund. Many people seem to have that impression, at least when they're starting out. Bad idea!

Your RRSP is actually a pension plan. In fact, it's the only one many of us will ever have apart from the Canada Pension Plan (CPP), which is universal, or the Quebec Pension Plan, if applicable. According to Statistics Canada, as of 2008 only 38 percent of workers in this country had an employer- or union-sponsored pension plan. Of those, the overwhelming majority were in the public sector. Only about one-quarter of private-sector workers were plan members.

So for most people, the RRSP is all they'll have to supplement the CPP and Old Age Security (OAS) when they retire.

This means you'd better pay close attention to that money. Your RRSP represents an investment portfolio, probably the largest one you'll ever have. You may have never thought of yourself as an investor, but the moment you open an RRSP you become one. How well you manage your money will have a significant impact on your lifestyle after retirement.

Here are some basic guidelines that will help you to build a plan that will provide a decent return on your money while keeping your assets reasonably safe:

Invest only in things you understand. The list of possible RRSP investments is long and ranges from the relatively simple, such as GICs, to the ultra-sophisticated, such as covered call options. Many people make the mistake of putting money into high-risk exotic investments that seem to offer big rewards. Usually the only ones who make money in such situations are the promoters. There's a very simple rule about investing that will never steer you wrong: If you don't understand it, don't put money into it.

Diversify your plan. Don't put all your RRSP eggs into one basket. The best-performing plans contain a mixture of securities—stocks, bonds, mutual funds, ETFs, etc. A diversified approach will improve your prospects for better returns while at the same time reducing your risks. But be disciplined—be aware of what you are doing and why. An asset mix approach is the best way to achieve this, and you'll find more on that later in this chapter.

Take the long view. You and your RRSP are going to be partners for a long time. Your investment strategy should reflect that. Virtually every decision you make should have at least a five-year horizon, with the exception of cash movements. That doesn't mean you should never sell a security you've held for less than five years, but you should have an extremely good reason for doing so. The biggest mistake most novice investors make is trading too frequently. That's costly and normally counterproductive. In most cases, you'll be much better off making sound investment decisions at the outset, and then holding the security for several years.

For example, I have owned shares of pipeline giant Enbridge in my RRSP/RRIF for a long time, through good years and bad. The company has a record of increasing its dividends each year, and the price of its shares has risen steadily. Between August 1999 and May 2013, the stock gained 828 percent in value, on top of the quarterly dividends. One share purchased back then at a price of $8 (split-adjusted) was yielding 15.75 percent by 2013. Yes, there were times over the years when it may have been tempting to sell, such as in the crash of 2008–2009. But sound, stable businesses can weather such storms. Build your RRSP with them, or with mutual funds that invest in them.

Keep costs low. Any money your RRSP spends on fees or commissions is lost to the plan forever. That's why you should keep such charges to a minimum. If you're purchasing mutual fund units, look for no-load funds or front-end load funds with zero commission (many brokers will waive their commission because they will collect trailer fees going forward). Do not use DSC units, which hit you with a sales commission if you sell before the holding period is over (usually seven years). Look for funds with low management expense ratios (MERs). Exchange-traded funds (ETFs) have much lower expenses than mutual funds, and the difference goes right to your bottom line. However, some mutual fund companies, such as Mawer, Steadyhand, and Beutel Goodman, keep their expenses at a minimum, and their funds often outperform comparable ETFs

Don't lose money. Billionaire Warren Buffett once said: "The first rule of investing is don't lose money. The second rule is don't forget rule number one." His advice is particularly appropriate for RRSPs. Since you can't replace any money lost as a result of bad investments, you should do everything in your power to protect your capital. If you do incur losses, keep them to a minimum. That means avoiding speculative investments and not selling high-quality securities if they go into a temporary slump because of corrections in the stock or bond markets.

Maximize compounding. There are two keys to building a million-dollar-plus RRSP. The first is to make regular contributions. The second is to invest in a way that your money will steadily compound over many years. Your plan should include securities that maximize the effect of compounding. The emphasis will vary depending on economic conditions, your age, your core strategy, and your risk tolerance level. Blue-chip stocks (e.g., banks, telecoms, utilities) will compound in value over time as we saw with Enbridge. During normal interest rate periods, fixed-income securities such as GICs and strip bonds will work nicely. I own a Bell Canada strip bond that I purchased for a RRIF for about $6000 back in 1991. When it matures in 2019, it will be worth $50,000. That's what compounding is all about.

Pay attention. Review your RRSP holdings at least once every three months to see how well they're performing and if any adjustments are required. You should also review every statement you receive from the company administering your RRSP. Errors creep into these reports occasionally; check to make sure that you've received credit for all interest and dividends and that the administrator's list of your assets corresponds with yours.

Contribute regularly. RRSP contributions shouldn't be determined by how much you have in your bank account in January or February. A regular contribution program, preferably on a monthly basis, will ensure your plan continues to grow at a steady rate and will eliminate the last-minute scramble for cash at deadline time. Many RRSPs now offer an automatic contribution plan, which enables you to authorize a specific amount for transfer from a savings or chequing account into your RRSP at regular intervals.

An Asset Mix Strategy

Repeated studies have shown that the most important single factor in investment returns is the blend of assets in your portfolio at any given time. This means that the types of investments you own, and the proportions in which you hold them, are much more critical to success than the individual securities you select. This is known as the asset mix, or asset allocation, approach to investing, and on average, it has been shown to account for some 80 percent (or more) of the performance of your RRSP over the years.

The right asset mix can reduce your risk and improve returns. Moreover, this approach to RRSP management is simple to understand and relatively easy to monitor. However, there is one caveat: You can't rely on asset mix alone to produce high-level returns. The quality of the individual securities you select for your retirement plan will also play a part in the results you achieve. If you fill your RRSP with junk, even the best asset mix in the world will produce mediocre to poor returns. That said, here's how the asset mix approach works.

There are three basic types of assets to consider. They are:

Cash and cash-equivalent. These are all the assets in your plan that are held either in cash form or in highly liquid securities (which means they can be quickly converted to cash with no loss of face value). The most common types of cash-equivalent securities held in RRSPs are:

- Canada Savings and Canada Premium bonds
- Term deposits (under six months)
- Treasury bills
- Bankers' acceptances
- Money market mutual funds
- High-interest savings accounts

Fixed-income securities. These are assets that pay a fixed rate of return for a specified period of time. Those most frequently held in retirement plans include:

- Bonds
- Conventional GICs
- Term deposits
- Strip bonds

Note that bond and mortgage mutual funds are technically not fixed-income securities because they do not guarantee a specific rate of return nor do they ever mature. It's the same for most ETFs, except the Target series from RBC, which do have maturity dates. Despite the fact that they aren't a perfect fit, bond mutual funds and ETFs are often used as fixed-income proxies because they are widely available and easy to buy.

Index-linked GICs also do not fit into this category. Although they have a maturity date, their returns are not guaranteed and depend on the performance of a benchmark, which could be a stock market index, a basket of shares or mutual funds, or something else. These securities are actually growth vehicles because the return depends on any increase in the value of the benchmark.

Growth securities. These are the rocket engine of your RRSP. They are the assets that will provide, through capital gains, the higher returns you need to ensure your RRSP will generate an above-average performance over time. The most common RRSP growth assets are:

- Common stocks
- Equity mutual funds (domestic and international)
- Real estate funds and REITs
- Gold

The way in which you combine these three asset groups will have a huge impact on the performance of your RRSP over time. You need to always be aware of what the mix is and be prepared to adjust it to meet changing economic conditions. For example, an RRSP that was heavily invested in fixed-income assets, such as government bonds, at the time of the 2008–2009 crash was much more effective in protecting assets than one that was overweighted in stocks and equity mutual funds.

As a general rule, it's a good idea to overweight fixed-income securities, especially bonds, at a time when interest rates are falling. When rates are on the rise, reduce bond positions and add to cash.

A heavy weighting in stocks or equity mutual funds/ETFs is likely to pay off handsomely during an economic recovery—as happened in 2009 in the rebound from the credit crash. Conversely, if you're overly committed to growth assets when equity markets turn down, your RRSP's performance will suffer, at least temporarily.

There are three basic principles you should apply when deciding on your asset mix:

1. *Broad diversification.* Don't heavily overweight your plan in any one security, sector, or country.

2. *Protection of capital.* If you suffer big losses along the way, it will severely compromise the amount of money that is available for your retirement. So take a conservative approach (keep in mind Warren Buffett's rules). Remember, this is a pension plan, not a gambling casino.

3. *Reduction of risk as you get older.* Many people had to postpone retirement after their savings were devastated by the 2008–2009 crash. That happened because their growth weighting was too heavy in relation to their age. Professional pension managers always hold a large percentage of their assets in bonds and similar securities. You should too. And the older you are, the higher that percentage should be.

Adding Stocks

The idea of including stocks in an RRSP terrifies some people. They regard them as far too risky, and the two stock market crashes we have experienced so far in this century (2000–2002 and 2008–2009) show that there is good reason for such anxiety. Those bear markets left deep psychological scars that are likely to endure for years to come. Many investors saw the value of their retirement plans tumble as market indexes collapsed.

This malaise has been compounded by global political uncertainty, a credit crisis that brought the world financial system to the brink of collapse, turbulence within the eurozone, and revelations of corporate misdeeds and false accounting practices by a few leading companies.

Yet amid all the uncertainty, there remains a strong case for everyone, even people who are retired and who hold a large part of their assets in income vehicles like RRIFs and LIFs, to have some exposure to the stock market. Whether you choose to invest in stocks directly or to hold them through mutual funds or ETFs, you should seriously consider including equities in your portfolio to the degree that is appropriate for your age and risk tolerance level. (See the next chapter for specific weighting suggestions.)

A longer-term perspective bears this out. Historically, stocks outperform cash, bonds, or inflation, and are likely to continue doing so in the future. That is not always the case, of course—bonds outperformed stocks by a wide margin in 2008. But these things have a way of balancing out. Over the long term, the stock market is an attractive investment from a risk/return perspective. If you have a self-directed plan, take advantage of the opportunity.

However, this does not mean you should load up your RRSP with junior mining stocks in the hope that one of them will make you rich. We're talking about a pension plan here, not a roulette wheel. Stick with sound, proven companies that have a history of regularly increasing their dividend payments. These include banks, utilities, pipelines, and similar stable businesses.

Don't hesitate to include some U.S. stocks in the mix.

Under the Canada–U.S. Tax Treaty, dividends paid by an American company into a retirement plan are not subject to the 15 percent withholding tax.

If you prefer to go the mutual fund route, look for well-managed value-oriented funds with a track record of above-average performance in weak markets.

For ETFs, choose only those that track a major index such as the Dow Jones Industrial Average or the S&P/TSX Composite Index. Don't get sidetracked with fringe funds that focus on specific sectors or countries; they can be volatile and unpredictable.

One advantage to blue-chip stocks that many people don't recognize is that they can actually generate more income than bonds or GICs when interest rates are low. At the time of writing, the maximum return available from a five-year GIC was only 3.15 percent. Shares of telecommunications giant BCE Inc., by contrast, were paying over 5 percent, plus they offered capital gains potential. These dividends can add decent cash flow to an RRSP or RRIF.

It's true that your stocks may suffer temporary setbacks. But if you choose wisely, they'll bounce back and the dividend will keep rolling in.

The odds are that stocks will do much better than bonds over the rest of this decade.

Just one caveat. If you have both a registered and a non-registered portfolio, you may want to consider keeping the stocks or equity funds outside the RRSP. That enables you to take advantage of the preferred tax rates for capital gains and dividends.

The Role of GICs

For years, GICs and term deposits were the mainstay of many RRSPs. Then a disaster happened—or at least it was a disaster from the point of view of the financial institutions that were growing wealthier from GIC sales. After hitting a 21st-century peak in late 2007, interest rates started falling to levels that had not been seen since the Great Depression. While it is not unusual for rates to decline during economic slowdowns, the extent of this drop and its duration were unprecedented in our lifetime. Some forecasters now predict low interest rates will be with us for the rest of this decade.

Low rates have made GICs an unattractive choice for all but the most conservative investors. Returns of 2 percent to 3 percent simply aren't cutting it for most people.

The marketing departments at the big banks have tried to stem the bloodletting by offering a range of sexier GICs that pay off depending on the performance of a particular stock index, mutual fund, or a basket of commodities. These are crapshoots, pure and simple. You could invest your money in them for as long as five years and get nothing back at the end of the day but your original capital. Your RRSP won't grow very quickly that way.

So are GICs even worth considering as long as interest rates remain low? The answer is a qualified yes, but you have to approach them strategically. The best course is to build a ladder of traditional, interest-paying GICs. This is simply a way of getting the best return from your fixed-income securities with minimal risk. The strategy can be used for GICs, bonds, and even some ETFs.

Here's how it works. Suppose you have $5000 you want to invest in fixed-income securities. You decide to use GICs. You do some research and discover that the highest rates are offered by some of the smaller banks and credit unions. That's all right as long as the GICs are covered by deposit insurance—ask first.

You build your ladder by investing $1000 in five separate GICs, maturing over five years. Using rates at the time of writing, here is what the ladder would look like:

$1000 for one year at 1.65 percent

$1000 for two years at 2.40 percent

$1000 for three years at 2.40 percent

$1000 for four years at 2.65 percent

$1000 for five years at 3.15 percent

During the first year, your ladder would return an average of 2.45 percent. At the end of the year, the first GIC matures. You roll it over into a new five-year certificate. Assuming interest rates remain unchanged, your ladder will now look like this:

$1000 for one year at 2.40 percent

$1000 for two years at 2.40 percent

$1000 for three years at 2.65 percent

$1000 for four years at 3.15 percent

$1000 for five years at 3.15 percent

The average return on your ladder is now up to 2.75 per cent. As you repeat the process each year, your return will increase as long as rates stay the same or move higher. And your RRSP money is never at risk because you will receive the face value of the GIC at maturity, plus accrued interest.

If you have a broker who is knowledgeable about the bond market, you can get a better return by creating a ladder of high-quality corporate bonds. They aren't covered by deposit insurance, but as long as the company remains solvent, you'll get your principal back at maturity. If you go this route, use only bonds rated BBB or higher.

For fans of exchange-traded funds, RBC offers a series of Target Maturity Corporate Bond ETFs that mature annually over the next several years. You can use them to construct an ETF ladder that could produce better returns than you'll get from GICs. But there is no deposit insurance coverage, no guarantee you'll get all of your principal back, and you will have to pay a brokerage commission to buy and sell the ETFs.

Whichever option you select, a ladder will optimize your fixed-income returns.

There's one more important point to remember when investing in GICs for your RRSP: Most bank and credit union managers have the discretion to improve on the posted rates. All you have to do is ask. They can usually give you up to a quarter-point more, but we've heard of bonuses of up to three-quarters of a percent where a lot of money was involved and the financial institution wanted to keep the business. So don't be afraid to do a little hard bargaining.

Mutual Funds

Mutual funds offer two major advantages: professional management and instant diversification. However, the fund universe is vast, and there are some very good and some very bad funds out there. Obviously, you want only the good ones for your RRSP. Here are some tips on what to look for:

Consistency. Look at the quartile ranking—how has the fund done over the years in relation to its peers? If it has not been in the first or second quartile at least 75 percent of the time, it is probably not worth considering (although there are occasional exceptions). You can find this information on several websites including GlobeInvestor, Morningstar Canada, and The Fund Library.

Reasonable return. To find whether the fund generates a reasonable profit, compare the rate of return against the category average over one, three, five, and ten years. If a fund is regularly outperforming its peers over time, it's a reasonable bet that pattern will continue and that you will receive above-average performance. No guarantees, of course, but unless there has been a managerial or mandate change, it's rare for a fund with a strong long-term record to suddenly start to underperform.

Good safety record. Apart from money market funds, very few funds have an unblemished safety record. So there is a degree of risk in every fund you buy. As a general rule, mortgage funds are the least risky, followed by bond funds, balanced funds, broadly based equity funds, and sector funds. Some websites offer risk metrics that enable you to assess a fund's volatility, number of losing periods, worst 12-month period, etc. Some company websites also have a volatility meter that enables you to see at a glance how the sponsor ranks a fund on the risk scale. These can all be helpful tools when making a final decision.

Low cost. High sales commissions and MERs will eat away at your returns. Look for funds that you can acquire at no cost and that have expense ratios below the category average.

A credible portfolio. All the fund websites include information on the largest positions in each fund. Some company sites go even further, providing lists of all the assets. It's worth checking at least the top ten to be sure you're getting what you want. If you're looking for a blue-chip fund and you don't recognize a single name among the largest positions, you'd better find an alternative.

Mutual funds can be a valuable addition to your RRSP but you need to devote a little time to researching the best choices. One final piece of advice on this: Don't buy one of the off-the-shelf fund portfolios that many financial institutions and advisers push. Based on the research I've done, they tend to be underperformers. In many cases, an ordinary balanced fund will do better.

6
RRSP Portfolios

Now that you understand the principles of asset allocation, it's time to use that knowledge to create some basic portfolios for your plan. Here are some suggestions that you can use as guidelines. Don't feel you have to rigidly adhere to them; everyone's goals and risk tolerance is different. But these models will help you to determine if you are on track or seriously off base. Note that these are asset mixes within an RRSP; your total portfolio, which includes non-RRSP investments, may have a slightly different look. A mutual fund, multi-purpose, or self-directed RRSP is required to implement these mixes.

Age 20–25

Asset type	Minimum allocation	Maximum allocation
Cash	5%	10%
Fixed income	40%	50%
Growth	45%	60%

At first glance, the fixed-income allocation in this portfolio may seem unusually high. However, there is method in my madness. Novice investors often make the mistake of taking on too much risk. They can end up suffering unnecessary losses because of this. Therefore, I suggest erring on the side of caution during the early years until you have a better understanding of the investing process. Once you are at that level, move to the next stage.

Age 26–50

Asset type	Minimum allocation	Maximum allocation
Cash	5%	10%
Fixed income	20%	50%
Growth	50%	70%

At this point, the RRSP becomes more growth-oriented so the emphasis will be on stocks and/or equity funds. But select wisely. Blue-chip stocks and the funds that invest in them will provide the best combination of steady returns and reasonable risk over time.

Don't be afraid to fine-tune the asset mix from time to time in line with economic conditions. For example, when stock markets hit record highs and you start hearing talk about a bubble, it might be time to take some equity profits and beef up the fixed-income side of the portfolio.

After you pass 50, it's time to start gearing down. You want to gradually reduce your stock market exposure while at the same time retaining some growth potential in the portfolio. Here's what the next stage might look like.

Age 51–60

Asset type	Minimum allocation	Maximum allocation
Cash	5%	15%
Fixed income	40%	60%
Growth	40%	55%

By increasing your cash and fixed-income assets, you lessen the potential damage that could be done to your RRSP by a stock market plunge. The more uncertain the times, the lower your growth component should be.

Assuming that you are aiming to retire around age 65 (although more people are working well past that age these days), this is what the RRSP should look like in the final run-up to retirement.

Age 61–65

Asset type	Minimum allocation	Maximum allocation
Cash	5%	20%
Fixed income	50%	70%
Growth	30%	40%

At this point, the plan is heavily weighted to cash/fixed-income, with the top priority being to protect the assets you have nurtured all these years. Note that the age range is arbitrary; this is the target mix you should be using until you actually stop work.

Now for one final table. Here's what your plan (which may be a RRIF at this stage) should look like once you have left the workforce.

Post-Retirement

Asset type	Minimum allocation	Maximum allocation
Cash	10%	20%
Fixed income	50%	75%
Growth	20%	30%

At this stage in your life, you'll need to increase the cash reserves to provide the income you'll be drawing from the plan. The growth component is down to between 20 percent and 30 percent, but it has not disappeared entirely—you need some growth potential to stay ahead of inflation. But choose only very conservative stocks or funds. Risk should be virtually eliminated at this stage since you will no longer be making contributions to the plan.

These models assume a person is just starting out. If you already have an RRSP, take a close look at what you've invested in and determine your current asset mix. See how it compares with the recommended range for your age and the current economic climate.

If you're underweighted in any one area, direct your next contribution to securities that will build your strength in that particular asset group. Many people may find that their RRSP is light on fixed-income assets. If that turns out to be the case, use at least a portion of this year's contribution to correct the problem, perhaps by investing in a GIC ladder. You can also use bond funds, even though, strictly speaking, they are not true fixed-income assets.

Once you've adjusted your asset mix to a level with which you're comfortable, monitor it at least quarterly to see if any modification is indicated, perhaps because of a change in the economic climate. To keep costs low, try to carry out any shifts by directing funds from new contributions to those asset groups that need to be increased. Alternatively, see if you can switch some of your holdings from one type of mutual fund (e.g., an equity fund) into another type of fund (e.g., a bond fund) within the same corporate family. This can sometimes (but not always) be done free or at a nominal charge.

If you maintain a proper asset mix and choose your investments wisely, your RRSP will pay big dividends for you over the years.

7
Mistakes to Avoid

Managing an RRSP is not easy. It requires discipline, knowledge, and that most precious commodity of all, time. For many people, the RRSP may eventually become their second most valuable asset, after the family home. And the amount of money you accumulate in the plan will one day become a major factor in determining how comfortable and stress-free your retirement years will be.

That's why it's so important to avoid making serious mistakes with your RRSP. They can cost you a lot of money— perhaps tens of thousands of dollars. Here are some of the most common errors I've encountered over the years:

Not having a plan. Most Canadians—and I stress the word most—should open an RRSP as soon as it is financially possible to do so. The majority of people in this country do not have a workplace pension plan. This means that their only certain sources of income in retirement are the OAS and the CPP or QPP. Even if you qualify for the maximum amount from both programs, that's only about $1560 a month (2013 rates) or less than $19,000 a year. If you can have the lifestyle you want on that amount, fine. Most people can't. Your RRSP will provide the difference between a subsistence existence and a comfortable retirement.

That said, there are a few situations in which having an RRSP is not a great idea. One example is an older person with a low income who is likely to be eligible for the Guaranteed Income Supplement (GIS) at age 65. Payments from an RRSP or RRIF are considered as income, so the GIS benefit will be reduced accordingly. These folks are better off using TFSAs because those withdrawals don't count as income.

Also, people with gilt-edged defined benefit pension plans—and there aren't very many of them—probably don't need an RRSP and won't have much contribution room in any event. In that situation, a TFSA is a better way to save.

Otherwise, you need to have an RRSP, and the sooner the better.

Choosing the wrong plan. Many people think one RRSP is the same as another. They don't appreciate that there are several different types of plans, each with its own built-in strengths and weaknesses. This is the type of person who dashes into a bank on the day before the RRSP deadline, writes a cheque on her account, and gives instructions to put it into an RRSP. If she doesn't specify the type of plan, the money will almost certainly be directed to a GIC, which provides a very limited return in a low interest rate environment. Review the chapter on the different types of RRSPs before making any decision on opening your account.

Not contributing. Often money is tight and making an RRSP contribution is somewhere near the bottom of the priority list. Lots of people have that problem, but here's my advice: Make a contribution every year, no matter how small. Get into the habit of growing your plan, even if you can only afford $100. Of course, making the maximum allowable contribution is the ideal choice, but not many people can afford that. So put in whatever you can.

To make the process easier, set up an automatic monthly contribution plan at your financial institution. Decide how much you can contribute for the year, divide that amount by 12, and have the required amount transferred directly from your chequing or savings account to your RRSP each month. Be sure you give clear instructions as to how your deposits should be invested; don't let them sit idly in cash.

Forgetting about it. Making an RRSP contribution isn't the end of the process. It's just the beginning. Yes, the tax deduction is very nice and you may be able to make good use of that extra cash. But what really matters over the long haul is how well you manage the money that you've put into the plan. It won't invest itself (unless you choose a GIC with an automatic rollover). It's up to you to make the decisions to ensure your RRSP money is working hard on your behalf.

This is especially important if you choose a mutual fund plan or a self-directed RRSP. Conditions change, new opportunities arise, once-successful mutual funds fall by the wayside—there are dozens of factors that can sharply reduce the returns on your registered plan. Remember, all the profits earned within your RRSP are tax-sheltered until the money comes out. You get to keep all of it. So do everything possible to manage the plan effectively and to maximize your return potential without incurring undue risk.

Playing roulette. Note the last four words of the preceding paragraph: "without incurring undue risk." Many people tend to treat the assets in their RRSP as Monopoly money. They know they won't have access to it for many years so they do silly things like chasing hot tips on the TSX Venture Exchange. This "go for the big score" rationale usually ends in large losses—money that cannot be replaced (the CRA does not allow extra contribution room for investment incompetence). Your RRSP should be conservatively managed, with capital preservation high on the priority list. If you want to gamble, do it outside your plan where, if you lose money, you can at least claim a capital loss for taxation purposes.

Trading too frequently. It costs money to buy and sell securities if your RRSP includes load mutual funds, stocks, REITs, ETFs, or any of a variety of other assets. These commissions must be paid from inside the plan. So it doesn't take a rocket scientist to figure out that if you do a lot of trading, a sizable portion of your capital is going to vanish over time. If your trading profits are high enough, perhaps you won't care. But if you are going to have a lot of this kind of activity, you'd better be good at it. Otherwise, select some sound securities for the long term and stay with them.

Ignoring your asset mix. As I explained in the last chapter, a well-thought-out asset allocation strategy is one of the best ways to ensure a successful RRSP portfolio. Some studies have found that having the proper asset allocation can account for more than 70 percent of a portfolio's returns, regardless of the specific securities selected (assuming they are not junk). Establish your allocation goals at the outset, and then review them at least twice a year to ensure you are on track.

Relying on the carry-forward. The best point about the carry-forward rule is that it allows you to make up for missed contributions. The worst is that it is often used as an excuse for not contributing at all. "Let's spend the money on a holiday. We'll make it up next year." The problem is that "making it up" often never happens. You'll find more on this topic in the next chapter.

Waiting until the last minute. It's actually become a joke: We have five seasons in Canada—spring, summer, fall, winter, and RRSP. Every January and February, people pour millions of dollars into their retirement plans in a last-minute scramble to beat the tax deadline. Where were they the rest of the year? The March 1 cut-off date doesn't come as a surprise—it's the same every year (except leap years, when the deadline is February 29, and years when the cut-off date falls on a weekend, when the government normally provides a day or two of grace). But that doesn't seem to matter. It's human nature to put things off to the end, especially if it involves investing money you'd rather use in some other way.

The problem is that this frantic rush can have several negative effects. For starters, it reduces the returns within your plan. Look at it this way: If you'd made your contribution several months earlier, the money would already be earning tax-sheltered income. Over time, that extra money can add up to thousands of dollars. A second problem is that last-minute deposits often mean hasty investment decisions—and rushed decisions can be bad decisions. So this year, plan to get the money (or at least part of it) in sooner, and take your time deciding where and how you want it invested. It will pay off in the long run.

Focusing too much on Canada. For the first decade of this century, Canada was one of the best places for your investment money. The Toronto Stock Exchange consistently outperformed its New York counterparts as resource stocks and funds flourished and financials did well. The crash of 2008–2009 wiped out some of those gains, but then markets rebounded in 2009–2010. As a result, many people kept most or all of their RRSP dollars at home, despite the removal of all foreign-content restrictions.

But all that changed after 2010. The economic slowdown dampened world demand for commodities, knocking down prices for copper, oil, iron ore, etc. and hitting the resource stocks accordingly. The Toronto Stock Exchange basically rests on two pillars: resources and financials. When one of them is kicked away, the market sags—which is exactly what happened. At the same time, the much more diverse American economy began to gather steam, driving U.S.

stocks higher. RRSP investors who owned shares in American equities, mutual funds, or ETFs prospered.

The point is that you need to diversify your RRSP not only by asset class but also geographically. If you have any securities in your plan other than GICs and savings accounts, make sure you include at least one U.S. and one international mutual fund or ETF.

Mismanaging the Home Buyers' Plan or Lifelong Learning Plan. Millions of Canadians tap into their RRSPs long before retirement for the down payment on a first home or to help finance higher education. It's nice to have an interest-free source of cash for these purposes, but it will cost you in the future by significantly reducing the amount of money in your plan when the time comes to retire. So think it through carefully before you make the decision to borrow from your RRSP, and if you do, try to pay back the money as quickly as possible.

Not naming a beneficiary. If you don't name a beneficiary, your RRSP will form part of your estate, which could result in probate fees and taxes. If you have a spouse/partner, that person should be the designated beneficiary of your plan. Should anything happen to you, this will allow for a quick and tax-free transfer of the money.

Making unnecessary withdrawals. I often receive questions from people asking whether it is a good idea to withdraw RRSP money to pay down debt, do home renovations, etc. Usually, the answer is no. Your RRSP is not a savings account, to be tapped into whenever quick cash is needed. It is a pension plan and should be treated accordingly. And remember that RRSP withdrawals are taxable. That means that if you are in a 40-percent tax bracket and need $10,000 to pay down a loan, you would actually have to withdraw $16,667 to end up with the amount you require, net of tax.

That's it. Avoid these mistakes, and your RRSP will prosper over the years. I guarantee it!

8
RRSP Strategies

So you've made your RRSP contribution and you've decided how you want the money invested. You're probably feeling rather satisfied with yourself, and rightly so. But there's more that needs to be done if you are going to get the most out of your retirement plan. Here are some strategies to consider. They won't apply in all cases, so choose the ones that work for you.

Avoid Using the Carry-Forward

Don't have the money to make an RRSP contribution this year? That's not a problem, at least in theory. You're allowed to carry forward unused contribution room indefinitely, so you can make it up any time in the future. But there's a price for doing that: It could end up costing you tens or even hundreds of thousands of dollars when the time comes to finally stop work.

Unused deduction room is calculated by determining your maximum allowable RRSP contribution for the year and then subtracting the amount you actually put into the plan. For example, if you have $10,000 in contribution room but only put in $3000, you have $7000 still available for future years.

Most people have carry-forward room available, often many thousands of dollars' worth. That's because few Canadians are able to make their maximum contribution each year. You can find out the exact amount you have available by going to the CRA website and clicking on "My Account."

In certain circumstances, the carry-forward can be a big help for people who want to increase their RRSP savings. Under the old use-it-or-lose-it rule, if you missed a contribution, the opportunity was gone forever. Now you have a chance to make up for it.

The downside of the carry-forward is that it can be an excuse for procrastination. In mid-February, with the RRSP deadline approaching, it's often tempting to think about hopping a plane and getting away from winter for a while. "We'll do the RRSP next year," you promise yourself. It's like a New Year's resolution—you mean it at the time but when next year comes around there's something else the money is needed for.

The result may be a build-up of more contribution room than you will ever realistically be able to use. Even if your income is relatively low, it won't take long to build a large bank of carry-forward credits. Suppose, for example, your earned income in 2014 is $40,000, and it increases at a rate of 2 percent a year for the next decade. You (like most Canadians) have no pension plan.

Your 2015 RRSP deduction limit is $7200 (18 percent × $40,000). You decide you'd rather spend the money on a holiday in Florida. You'll make it up next year, you promise yourself. But then something else comes up and you put it off again. This goes on for the next 10 years. Here's how your carry-forward room will build:

Year	Carry-forward room
2015	$ 7200
2016	$14,544
2017	$22,035
2018	$29,683
2019	$37,477
2020	$45,426
2021	$53,534
2022	$61,805
2023	$70,241
2024	$78,846

The danger is obvious. By 2024, you'll have built up almost $79,000 in unused RRSP deduction room. But your annual salary at that point is less than $48,000. Your unused deduction limit is almost double the amount you earn in a full year! How likely is it you will ever be in a position to make up for all those missed contributions?

That's only part of the downside. If you don't make an RRSP contribution, you'll lose the tax deduction that comes with it. And while RRSP contributions are currently treated as deductions, that may not always be the case. A future government may decide to convert them to tax credits, which would have the effect of reducing the refund they generate for everyone but those in the lowest tax bracket. Tax credits are different from tax deductions in that you get to deduct only a set percentage of the expense—rather than the whole amount—against your taxable income.

The final point to consider is that using the carry-forward will reduce the end value of your RRSP. The longer the money grows in your plan tax-free, the greater the final value will be. Using the carry-forward compromises this advantage by reducing the number of years of tax-sheltered compounding available to you. Even the loss of a few years can make a big difference to the value of your plan, especially if it occurs when you're relatively young.

Take the case of a 30-year-old who contributes $5000 to his RRSP for the 2014 tax year and who hopes to retire at age 65. If he makes the contribution this year and the money is invested in a diversified portfolio that earns 6 percent annually, the $5000 will grow to about $38,400 when the time comes to retire.

But suppose he decides to use the carry-forward and delays contributing the money for five years. At age 35, he finally gets around to it. Again, assuming growth in the RRSP at 6 percent a year, his $5000 contribution will only be worth about $28,700 when he retires. In other words, the five-year delay has reduced the final value of his RRSP by almost $10,000!

Remember that the higher the projected return on your RRSP investments, the greater the cost if you use the carry-forward.

The bottom line is: Use the carry-forward if you must, but if you do, try to make up the shortfall as soon as possible.

Defer Claiming the Deduction

One of the little-known RRSP rules is that you are not required to claim a deduction in the same year you make a contribution. Deductions, like contribution room, can be carried forward and used at a more advantageous time.

This can be a valuable strategy in years when income is low and the value of a tax deduction would therefore be minimal. Here are two examples.

In the first case, let's look at Jim, who graduated from university with an engineering degree in May. He immediately landed an entry-level job with a major construction firm. His initial salary isn't very high, but given his education and people skills, his future prospects are excellent.

After taking the summer off to travel, Jim starts his new job after Labour Day. He realizes the importance of starting a savings plan early, so he opens an RRSP and arranges to have monthly contributions deducted from his bank account. As a result, he accumulates $2000 in deductions during the four months he works in that year.

However, because he has only been employed for a short period, he is in the lowest tax bracket (15 percent at the federal level). If he claims the deduction immediately, it will generate a very small refund. Therefore, he decides to defer claiming the deduction until a future year when his income will be higher and it will save him more tax dollars.

This strategy works because RRSP deductions are subtracted from your other earnings before your taxable income is calculated (see line 208 of the federal return).

This means that you save an amount equal to your marginal tax rate.

In this case, let's assume Jim's marginal tax rate (federal and provincial) during his first year of employment, when he worked only four months, was 15 percent. If he claimed the $2000 deduction, he would save only $300. But the following year, when he is working full time, his income triples and his marginal tax rate rises to 25 percent. Now that same $2000 deduction saves him $500 on his tax bill. He gains an extra $200 by waiting.

The same approach can also be used for teenagers who work during the summer. If they have earned income, they can open an RRSP and make a small contribution. The deduction can then be deferred for several years until such time as they can make better use of it.

Next, let's consider the case of Susan. Her mother passed away in April, leaving her entire estate to her daughter, including an insurance policy worth $100,000. As a result, Susan decides to take a leave of absence from her job to spend more time with her two children, who were very upset by their grandmother's death.

Susan had accumulated $15,000 in RRSP carry-forward credits before all this happened. She decides to use some of the insurance money to top up her plan, thus creating a large amount of deduction room. But since her income that year will be very low because of the leave of absence, she would be smart to delay claiming that deduction until she goes back to work full time.

Delaying an RRSP deduction to maximize tax savings is perfectly legal, but many people fail to take advantage of this strategy. Take a close look at your own situation. It could save you a lot of money.

Consider a Contribution in Kind

Don't have the cash to make an RRSP contribution this year? You're not alone. However, you may be able to contribute anyway and earn a tax deduction in the process. If you have any investments that are not already in a registered plan, such as GICs, mutual funds, or stocks, you can make what is known as a "contribution in kind."

Any qualified security can be put directly into an RRSP, within the usual contribution limits. You'll receive full credit for a tax deduction at the security's current market value, so this strategy can be extremely valuable if you're short of cash at RRSP time. However, contributions in kind are only possible with a self-directed plan.

For example, suppose you have $5000 invested in a GIC that doesn't mature for three years. You can't cash it in, but you're short of money for this year's RRSP contribution. If you have a self-directed plan, you can simply contribute the GIC to it. You'll receive credit both for the principal amount and all compound interest earned up to that time. If the interest rate is 3 percent and you've held the certificate for two years, you'll actually receive credit for $5,304.50 when you make the contribution. Make sure you don't end up overcontributing to your RRSP by failing to take your accrued interest into account.

Here's another example. Suppose you have mutual fund units that have done well. You haven't held them the requisite seven years for the DSC to run down to zero, so you don't want to sell them just yet—but you need money for this year's RRSP contribution. As an alternative, you could contribute the units directly to the self-administered plan. The amount of your contribution will be based on the market value of the units on the day they go into your RRSP.

There are tax implications you should be aware of, however. Any time you make a contribution in kind to an RRSP, the CRA takes the position that you've sold the security. If the asset has increased in value since you bought it, you'll have a capital gain.

For example, if you paid $5000 for the fund units and they have a market value of $7000 when you put them into an RRSP, the government will take the position that you have a capital gain of $2000. You must declare this on your return and pay the appropriate tax.

Don't use this approach with securities that have declined in value. That's because, while any capital gain you make in this situation is taxable, the CRA won't allow you to claim a capital loss. In this case, you're better off selling the security and using the cash from the sale for your RRSP contribution. That way you'll be able to claim the loss on your tax return, as long as it can be offset against other capital gains.

The capital gain/loss rules won't apply to securities such as GICs because their value is fixed—they usually have no potential for capital gains or losses. Any increase in their value is normally related to compound interest and is taxed accordingly. Obviously, you'll have to declare any interest earned on your GICs up to the time they went into your retirement plan.

To summarize, here are the rules for RRSP contributions in kind:

1. You must have a self-directed RRSP to make contributions in kind.
2. The security must be a qualified investment.
3. The security must be contributed at fair market value.
4. Any accrued interest will form part of the contribution.
5. A contribution in kind will produce a tax deduction in the same way as a cash contribution.
6. The total value of the securities, including accrued interest, may not exceed your normal RRSP contribution limit.
7. Contributing a security that has increased in value since you acquired it will trigger a capital gain that must be declared on your income tax return.
8. You should not contribute a security that has decreased in value since being acquired, as this will result in a non-claimable capital loss.

Look at RRSP Loans

Going into debt to invest is rarely a good idea, but there are times when it can make sense. Borrowing to make your maximum RRSP contribution is one of those times, but the circumstances have to be right. There are three specific conditions you should meet:

1. You don't have adequate cash available and have no securities that you can use to make a contribution in kind.
2. You can repay the loan within one year. This is very important. Do not, under any circumstances, borrow money to make an RRSP contribution and then let the loan sit unpaid for years. You may end up paying more in non-deductible interest charges than you'll save on your tax refund. Plus, you'll have an unpaid debt hanging over your head that could come back to haunt you in years to come.
3. Using the carry-forward provision would not be to your advantage.

If all these conditions apply, borrowing for an RRSP is certainly worth considering. Here's an example to illustrate why.

Suppose you're entitled to make a maximum RRSP contribution of $5000 but you've only saved $2000. The contribution deadline is looming, and you're debating whether to contribute just $2000 or to borrow an extra $3000. Let's assume that your marginal tax rate is 40 percent, that you expect to get a 5 percent return on the mutual fund you're considering, and that the loan is repayable in 12 monthly instalments at an interest rate of 3.5 percent (RRSP loans are normally offered at prime rate or close to it). Here's how the alternatives work out.

If you decide to contribute only $2000, you'll receive a tax deduction of $800 ($2000 × 40 percent). Plus you'll earn $100 in the first year ($2000 × 5 percent) for a total return of $900 on your money.

Now let's assume you decide to borrow $3000 and contribute a total of $5000 to the plan, which you invest in the same mutual fund. You receive a tax deduction of $2000 ($5000 × 40 percent) plus $250 from your mutual fund investment for a total of $2250. However, you have to deduct the cost of the loan from your gain. Assuming you repay it over one year in monthly instalments of $254.76, your total interest cost will be only $57.18. Your net gain on the transaction will be $2192.82 compared to only $900 if you had decided against the loan and contributed just $2000.

And this assumes you make no prepayment against the principal over the year. If you use your $2000 tax refund as soon as it arrives to pay it down, your actual borrowing costs will be much less.

No matter what tax bracket you're in, the one-year return from borrowing for your RRSP will be greater than if you fail to make your full contribution, assuming you borrow the money at commercial rates. The higher your tax bracket, the greater the advantage of using this strategy. Just remember, the loan must be repaid within a year. In the second year, the costs of carrying the loan might be higher than the income the money earns inside the RRSP, and there are no more offsetting tax deductions.

Most financial institutions offer RRSP loans at favourable rates during the January/February period. Not all companies promote them, however, so you may have to do some investigating to find the best deals. Remember that interest charges for RRSP loans are not tax deductible, unlike interest payments on regular investment loans.

Roll Over Retiring Allowances

The term "retiring allowance" can be somewhat misleading. It actually covers a variety of payments. These include money you receive when you retire, in recognition of years of service to an organization. In this form, it may include payments relating to sick-leave credits you never claimed.

But a retiring allowance can be a euphemism for severance pay—money you received because you lost your job, for whatever reason.

Retiring allowances do not include any pension benefits, death payments, or benefits received for counselling services that are part of a termination arrangement.

Any eligible payments may be transferred directly to an RRSP (or to a RPP, but not to a RRIF) without being taxed, within certain limits. The transfer can be done in one of two ways:

1. By arranging to have the money transferred directly into your RRSP. In this type of arrangement, you avoid having income tax deducted at source. Your company's payroll department will handle this; just let them know that you have the contribution room.
2. By receiving the money yourself and making a contribution to your RRSP within 60 days of year-end. In this case, tax will be withheld on the payments when you receive them, but you'll get part or all of the money back when you file your return, depending on how much goes into the RRSP. To make a claim, show the total amount of the retiring allowance you received on line 130 of your return. You can then claim a deduction for the amount transferred to an RRSP at line 208. Be sure to attach a receipt for this amount to your return.

The maximum amount of eligible retiring allowances you can transfer directly to an RRSP without having contribution room available is $2000 times the number of years or part-years you were with the employer, up to and including 1995. No credit will be granted for any year or part-year from 1996 forward. You may also claim an additional $1500 for each year or part-year prior to 1989 for which no money was vested for you in a pension plan or DPSP. The formula looks like this:

($2000 × Years of service before 1996) + ($1500 × Non-pension years before 1989) = Eligible retiring allowance

For purposes of this calculation, any part of a calendar year is considered a full year. So, if you joined a company in July 1990 and left in July 2013, you're considered to have been with the firm for 24 years, not 23, as it might appear. However, since no credit is granted for service from 1996 to 2013, you may use only six years—1990 to 1995—as the basis for your calculation. As an example, if you had been with an employer from 1980 until 2013 and had no pension plan, your maximum retiring allowance eligible for an RRSP rollover would be:

$$(\$2000 \times 15) + (\$1500 \times 9) = \$30,000 + \$13,500 = \$43,500$$

If you were fully vested in the company pension plan for all those years, your maximum would be:

$$\$2000 \times 15 = \$30,000$$

But what about the portion of a retiring allowance that is not considered to be eligible for direct RRSP transfer? With eligibility only available for years up to 1995, many people find themselves faced with a heavy tax bite on these lump-sum payments. Fortunately, there is a solution—if you have contribution room in your RRSP, perhaps as a result of carry-forwards. If you provide evidence that you have unused contribution room, your employer may agree (note the word "may") to transfer an equivalent sum from a retiring allowance directly into your RRSP, without deducting tax. There is no obligation on employers to do this, however, and it's up to you to provide the evidence.

Here's an example of how this might work. We'll use a fictional retiree named Bill. He gets a retiring allowance of $50,000 in recognition of long service. Of this, Bill can transfer $21,000 directly to an RRSP by applying the credits available for service prior to 1996. He also has $10,000 in unused RRSP deduction room available and asks his boss to also transfer that amount to the plan. The amount subject to tax deductions at source will be:

Retiring allowance: $50,000
Amount eligible for direct transfer: $21,000
Amount transferred based on contribution room: $10,000
Total transferred to RRSP: $31,000
Amount taxed at source: $19,000

The employer does not require a letter of authority from the CRA to do this. Of course, if you've used all your contribution room, this option won't be available.

Make a Small Overcontribution

You are actually allowed to have a little more money in your RRSP than your legal contribution limit. Tax rules permit an extra $2000 in the plan without any penalty. But note: This $2000 is a lifetime, not annual, limit.

It may not seem like a lot, but over time that extra $2000 can give a nice little boost to your final nest egg. Let's say you add that amount early in life, when you're 25. You invest the money in a mutual fund that generates an average annual return of 5 percent. By the time you reach age 65, that $2000 has grown to a little more than $14,000. It's a nice bonus.

Just be careful not to exceed the $2000 limit. Beyond that, the CRA will assess a penalty of 1 percent per month until you withdraw the excess from the plan.

Analyze Your Group RRSP

Many employers now offer group RRSPs instead of pension plans. The advantages from their perspective are obvious: less expense and less paperwork. But for employees, it's not such a great deal, for several reasons.

First, no one else can contribute to your RRSP. That includes your employer. In a few cases, companies will offer extra compensation to help defray the RRSP contribution but that's rare. Usually, the employer simply makes the plan available and that's it.

Second, any contribution made to a group RRSP comes off your total limit for the year. There's no additional room. So if your total contribution limit is $10,000 and $7000 goes into the group plan, you have only $3000 remaining for your personal RRSP.

Third, group RRSPs offer a limited number of investment options. With your own plan, you can put the money into anything you want, from GICs to blue-chip stocks.

So why bother to join a group RRSP at all? There are a couple of reasons. For one, regular payroll deductions for plan contributions will reduce the amount of withholding tax from your salary. In effect, you'll be receiving some of your tax refund early. Also, payroll contributions provide a disciplined way of RRSP saving—you won't have to scramble at year-end to find the money you need.

A few employers offer both defined contribution pension plans and group RRSPs. In those cases, the investment options are usually the same, so if you take the time to study them you can use similar strategies in both accounts.

If a group RRSP is offered, find out all the details and the investment options before signing up. Once you've had a chance to study the details, you will be able to make an informed decision on whether to join or stick with a personal plan.

9
The Home Buyers' Plan

Way back in 1992, the government of Brian Mulroney introduced a bill to create the Home Buyers' Plan (HBP) to enable people to borrow from their RRSP to help finance a first home. It was supposed to be a temporary measure to help stimulate the housing market, which was in the midst of a terrible slump. More than two decades later the HBP is still with us, and millions of Canadians have used it to become homeowners. At this point, it's safe to say its popularity has made it a permanent RRSP feature—no government would dare to repeal it now.

Adoption of the plan set an important precedent. For the first time, people were allowed to draw funds from their RRSP for purposes other than retirement. And in this case, they were allowed to do so tax-free!

The basic concept of the program is simple. You are allowed to borrow up to $25,000 from an RRSP to purchase a home (so $50,000 for a couple). The money comes out as an interest-free loan that must be repaid over 15 years. Easy enough—it's the fine print that sometimes makes the plan more complicated. Here are the rules you need to know:

Eligibility. Technically, you are supposed to be a first-time homebuyer to use this plan. But there are so many loopholes in the rule that the HBP is available to many people who might be under the impression they can't use it. Essentially, you are considered to be a first-time buyer if neither you nor your spouse/partner has owned a home that you both occupied in the previous four years.

The actual wording in the guide to the HBP published by the CRA is that you don't qualify if you "owned a home that you occupied as your principal place of residence at any time during the period beginning January 1 of the fourth year before the year of the withdrawal and ending 31 days before the date of the withdrawal." So if you did not own a property on January 1, 2010, you would be eligible to use the HBP in 2014. The fact that you may have been a homeowner prior to that doesn't matter.

The same wording applies for a spouse/partner with the additional proviso that you both occupied the home. In real-world terms, this means if you are getting married to a homeowner and have not been living together, you can use the HBP to help finance the purchase of a new home. However, your future spouse would not be eligible.

Among the other key conditions are that you must have a written agreement to buy or build a home that will be used as your principal residence. The home must be bought or built by October 1 of the year following the withdrawal (so if you take out the money in 2014, the home must be ready by October 1, 2015). Also, you must be a resident of

Canada, and you cannot have any outstanding balance from a previous HBP loan.

You can bypass the first-time buyer rule if you are disabled and need a home better suited to your needs, or if you are withdrawing the money to purchase a home that will accommodate the needs of a disabled relative.

Note: Neither you nor your spouse can own the home more than 30 days prior to the withdrawal. So don't buy the house first and decide to use the HBP later. You'll be disqualified.

Qualifying home. Only a principal residence qualifies, and the home must be in Canada. No seasonal homes allowed. Existing and new homes are eligible, as are condos and even mobile homes. However, you can't use the money to pay down an existing mortgage or to renovate your present home. There is no minimum period of time you must live in the house once you occupy it.

How to apply. The application procedure is very simple. This program has a minimum of red tape attached, at least on the application side. Ask for form T1036, Home Buyers' Plan (HBP) Request to Withdraw Funds from an RRSP, at your District Taxation Office or download it from the CRA website at www.cra-arc.gc.ca/E/pbg/tf/t1036/t1036-12e.pdf, or call 1-800-959-2221 and ask for a copy.

Maximum withdrawal. You are allowed to take out $25,000 per person. If both members of a couple (either legally married or living common law, both opposite and same sex) have a retirement plan, they can take out up to $50,000 between them. You may also make withdrawals from a spousal RRSP without penalty, even if you've made a contribution to the plan within the last three years. The entire withdrawal must be made within the same calendar year.

Interest charges. None. This is an interest-free loan to yourself. It's the cheapest source of financing you can get, and it may save you thousands of dollars in mortgage insurance fees if the loan gives you enough money to qualify for a conventional mortgage.

Withholding tax. None. These withdrawals come out of your RRSP tax-free.

Repayment. You have 15 years to repay the loan, starting in the second year after you make the withdrawal. You have up to 60 days in the year following to do this—the same deadline as for regular RRSP contributions. So if you enter the plan in 2015, your first payment will be due in 2017, but you don't have to actually get the money into the plan until March 1, 2018. Repayment may be made to any RRSP you hold, not necessarily to the one from which you borrowed the money. You'll receive a notice from the CRA telling you how much you need to repay each year.

There are certain types of RRSP contributions that may not be used for HBP repayments. These include contributions to spousal plans, amounts transferred from a pension plan, and any amount for which you claim a tax deduction.

Extra payments. You may repay more than the minimum amount at any time, and it is in your best interest to do so, for reasons I'll explain below. The balance owing in each subsequent year will be adjusted accordingly.

Maturing RRSP. If you turn 71 before the loan is fully paid, you have three options. The first is to repay the balance owing before you convert your RRSP to a RRIF or annuity. The second is to make a partial repayment, while the third is to make no payment at all. If you choose option two or three, you must include in each subsequent year's income the payment that would have been due in that year (until the loan is repaid), and pay tax accordingly. The CRA will make that calculation for you.

Notification. The CRA will send a statement of your HBP account along with your annual notice of assessment. This shows, among other things, the amount of the payment due in the following year. You can also review your HBP status by using the My Account feature on the CRA website.

Death. It's not something you want to contemplate, but it's important to know that if you die, the amount owing on your HBP loan will be treated as income on your final return and taxed accordingly.

Leaving Canada. If you move to another country before an HBP loan is paid off, you must either repay the full amount or show the balance owing as income on your final Canadian tax return.

Tax filing. Anyone with an HBP loan must file a tax return each year, even if there's no income to report. The return enables the CRA to keep tabs on whether the loan is being repaid to the RRSP on schedule.

Penalties. Any payments not made on time will be treated as taxable withdrawals in the year they were due. You'll be assessed tax at your marginal rate on the amount that should have been repaid.

RRSP deductions. You may use the HBP and still claim a full RRSP deduction in that year, as long as the loan is not taken out within 90 days of contributing to your RRSP.

If you withdraw the money before the 90-day waiting period, special rules apply. Here's an example. Let's say you contribute $5000 to an RRSP on February 1. On April 15 (less than 90 days later), you withdraw $5000 from the RRSP by using the HBP. To calculate your allowable RRSP deduction, you subtract the fair market value of the assets remaining in the RRSP right after the withdrawal from the amount of the contribution.

Let's say your RRSP is brand new and the $5000 you deposited was the only asset. The value of the plan after the HBP loan would be nil, so you could not claim a deduction. However, if the plan had already been established for some time, it would be a different story. Let's assume the same scenario, except in this case the value of the assets left after the loan is $15,000. In this case, you can claim the full $5000 RRSP deduction at tax-filing time.

If you cannot wait 90 days before withdrawing the money, you can use the chart on the following web page to calculate the amount of RRSP deduction you can claim: www.cra-arc. gc.ca/E/pub/tg/rc4135/rc4135-e.html#calculation.

Talking Points

Before you apply for an HBP loan, there are a number of things to consider. For starters, does your RRSP have enough cash? Your total assets may be worth several thousand dollars, but can you get at them? If the money is tied up in locked-in GICs, perhaps not. Or if it's invested in mutual funds with a deferred sales charge, the commissions that will kick in when you sell may make the process quite expensive.

You'll need to have a discussion with the company holding your RRSP to determine how much cash is available for the program. Some financial institutions will allow participants to cash in GICs early, but there are often conditions attached. In some cases, this privilege is only available if you place the mortgage with the financial institution that holds your RRSP. Other companies may charge a penalty for early GIC termination.

Once you've determined that the cash is available, the next question to address is the hidden cost involved in using the plan. As with every financial decision, you'll be making a trade-off. In this case, you will have to sacrifice future retirement revenue for the benefit of owning a home right now because you'll lose the tax-sheltered income you would have earned if the money had stayed in the plan. The younger you are when you take an HBP loan, the greater the potential impact on the future value of your RRSP because of the effect of compounding.

However, the reduced value of the RRSP at retirement may be offset by a combination of mortgage interest savings, the appreciation in the value of your property over time, and some smart investment strategies. Also, repaying the loan ahead of schedule will reduce the impact on your retirement capital.

But even if using the HBP costs you some retirement income, it may still be worth going ahead in order to improve your lifestyle. Years ago, my oldest daughter asked for my advice on whether to use the program. At the time, she and her husband lived in a one-bedroom rented apartment and had a baby on the way. They had very little savings except for her RRSP.

I didn't hesitate in telling her to apply. Yes, she might have less retirement capital when she stops work, but money is only a means to an end—that end being to live comfortably, in a lifestyle that suits us. They needed a home and they needed it right away. The numbers didn't matter. In fact, if they'd had to live in their tiny apartment with a squalling baby, they probably wouldn't have made it to retirement anyway! Keep that in mind when it comes time to make your decision.

Although younger people are most likely to use the HBP,

it can also be valuable for older Canadians. At a seminar several years ago, a 71-year-old woman who was living in a rented apartment asked if the plan made sense for her. It certainly did! She had to wind up her RRSP within the year in any event. The HBP enabled her to take out $25,000 immediately to buy a home, while deferring taxes on part of that amount until well into the future. At one stroke, she got access to a large amount of cash and eliminated her exposure to rising rental costs. Since she no longer had an RRSP when repayments were due to start, she paid taxes on one-fifteenth of the amount she borrowed each year. Since she was in a low tax bracket, those taxes would be minimal. In her case, it was a great deal.

The whole idea of using retirement savings for other purposes was certainly not the intent of the policy-makers at the time RRSPs were created. But the HBP has now become a part of Canada's personal finance fabric, and it's safe to say that a lot of people would be living in rental accommodation today had it not been introduced.

It's important to understand the implications of the plan and the effect it will have on your retirement savings if you use it. But in the end it comes down to your personal priorities. If owning a home now is at the top of your list and the HBP is the only way to achieve that, go ahead.

10
The Lifelong Learning Plan

The success of the Home Buyers' Plan inspired federal lawmakers to devise another way for Canadians to take money from their RRSPs for what were deemed to be worthwhile reasons.

The Lifelong Learning Plan (LLP) was unveiled in the 1998 federal budget. Since January 1, 1999, Canadians have been given the option of borrowing from their RRSPs to help pay the costs of post-secondary education. The stated goal is to provide an alternative means of raising capital to allow people to upgrade their skills in order to retain their current job or obtain a new one. The rationale is that retraining or further education is often vital to ensuring future employment income and, subsequently, retirement income.

Unfortunately, as with the HBP, the federal government has made no effort to educate Canadians as to the very real cost of using the LLP. As with the HBP, if you don't adopt a strategy to offset the loss of capital in your RRSP, the end result may be a much-diluted capital base when it comes time to retire.

Here are the key points of the LLP:

Eligibility. Any Canadian resident with an RRSP may apply. The funds must be used to finance full-time training or education for the plan holder or his or her spouse/partner. The individual must enrol as a full-time student in a qualifying educational program at an eligible educational institution. If the funds are withdrawn before enrolment, the enrolment must occur in the year of withdrawal or, at the latest, before March of the following year.

The CRA defines an eligible educational institution as a university, college, or other educational facility that qualifies for claiming the education tax credit. For more details, check out their pamphlet titled *Students and Income Tax*.

A qualifying program must be at least three months in length and must require the student to spend at least 10 hours a week in lectures or on course work. Also, the student must be designated as "full-time" by the school itself.

Students with disabilities may qualify for the LLP even if they are only registered for part-time courses. The CRA says this rule can be used by students who qualify for the disability tax credit or who "cannot reasonably be expected to be enrolled as a full-time student because of a mental or physical impairment." In such cases, a certificate from an appropriate medical practitioner must accompany form T2202.

Children's education. You cannot use the LLP to help pay the education costs of your children or grandchildren, or the children/grandchildren of your spouse/partner.

How to apply. Use form RC96, titled Lifelong Learning Plan (LLP) Request to Withdraw Funds from an RRSP. You can download it at www.cra-arc.gc.ca/E/pbg/tf/rc96/README. html or call 1-800-959-2221 and ask for a copy.

Withdrawal period. You may make withdrawals for four successive calendar years. So if you make the first withdrawal in 2015, you have until February 2019 to complete the cycle.

Maximum withdrawal. The annual limit is $10,000. There is no restriction on the number of withdrawals in any given year or the number of RRSP accounts involved, as long as the annual limit is not exceeded. The maximum amount allowed during a given "withdrawal period" may not exceed $20,000. Individuals may participate more than once in their lifetime. However, people in the repayment portion of the program cannot make further withdrawals or begin another cycle until the total amount owing from the previous loan has been repaid.

Independently, your spouse/partner may also withdraw the same amounts from his/her RRSP, thereby potentially doubling the amount available for education purposes.

Spending limitations. None. One of the interesting aspects of this program is that the money does not have to be used for tuition, books, or indeed for any educational purpose. As long as the qualifying conditions are met, the government does not require proof that the loan was in fact used for education. So a person on a full scholarship could make use of the LLP to borrow money interest-free for any purpose.

Interest charges. None. This is an interest-free loan to you from your RRSP.

Withholding tax. None. These withdrawals come out of your RRSP tax-free.

Repayment. A minimum of one-tenth of the amount withdrawn annually is repayable to any RRSP you have, so you must repay the loan over a period of not more than 10 years. This means that the loan does not necessarily have to be repaid to the plan from which you borrowed the money originally.

The CRA determines when the repayment period starts by checking line 322 of your tax return to see if you were entitled to the education amount as a full-time student for at least three months. If you do not meet this condition two years in a row, your repayment period usually starts in the second of those two years. However, if you continue to meet this condition every year, your repayment period starts in the fifth year after your first LLP withdrawal.

Extra payments. You may pay back more than the minimum required amount at any time. It's a good idea to do this if possible—getting the money back into the RRSP early will increase the amount of tax-sheltered compounding in the plan and reduce the ultimate loss to your retirement capital.

Maturing RRSP. If you turn 71 before the loan is fully paid, you have three options. The first is to repay the balance owing before you convert your RRSP to a RRIF or annuity. The second is to make a partial repayment, while the third is to make no payment at all. If you choose option two or three, you must include in each subsequent year's income the payment that would have been due in that year (until the loan is repaid), and pay tax accordingly. The CRA will make that calculation for you.

Notification. You will receive a statement of your LLP account from the CRA each year with your notice of assessment. It will show your total withdrawals, your current loan balance, the amounts you have repaid to date, and the amount you have to repay the following year. You can also review your LLP status by using the My Account feature on the CRA website.

Quitting school. Special rules apply if you decide you don't want to complete the educational program. If you quit before April of the year after you make the withdrawal, you can still make your repayments over a 10-year period if less than 75 percent of your tuition is refunded. If more than 75 percent is paid back, you have to cancel the LLP withdrawal entirely. This means the money needs to be repaid to the RRSP.

The CRA will keep tabs on whether you are still in school by checking the education amount claimed on line 322 of your tax return. If you don't make the claim, or if it seems too low to qualify, expect a phone call from a tax collector.

Death. If the student dies before the LLP loan is repaid in full, a surviving spouse/partner can choose to continue to make repayments to an RRSP rather than have the amount owing included in the deceased person's final tax return. To do this, the survivor and a lawyer must sign a letter indicating such an election has been made and attach it to the deceased's final return. This can be done even by survivors who have their own LLP balance owing.

Leaving Canada. If you become a non-resident, you must repay any LLP loan in full to your RRSP before departing or include the amount owing as income when you file your final Canadian return.

Tax filing. You must file a tax return for every year you participate in the program and until the loan is fully repaid. This is required even if your income is very low and you don't owe any tax. You will need to complete schedule 7 of the return to show any withdrawals or repayments made during the year. For the first year, indicate in part E if your spouse/partner is the student, otherwise the CRA will assume it is you.

Penalties. Any part of the required amount that is not repaid in the year it is due will be included in computing your income for that year. In other words, you'll end up paying tax on it.

RRSP deductions. No deduction will be allowed for RRSP contributions made less than 90 days before the funds are withdrawn under the plan. (See this topic in chapter 9 for more details on how this rule is applied.)

Talking Points

As with the HBP, there are a number of factors to consider before you withdraw RRSP funds to finance continuing education for yourself or your spouse/partner.

First, does your RRSP have enough cash? Many individuals hold investments other than cash in their plan and would have to sell assets to finance the withdrawal. Review whether this is a wise decision from an investment perspective, giving consideration to fees incurred and your long-term plan. Also, you may find that some of your holdings, such as non-redeemable GICs, cannot be converted to cash until maturity.

You must also consider the long-term effects of withdrawing funds from your RRSP, specifically the impact on the assets you will ultimately have available for retirement. Every year the funds remain out of your RRSP costs you tax-free compounding that can never be recovered. As explained in the Home Buyers' Plan chapter, this loss could result in a significant reduction in your retirement income.

The upside is that improving your education could result in an increase in employment income that will offset any lost retirement income from the original LLP withdrawal.

In addition to the numbers, you should also consider quality of life and the career choices that would be available should you choose not to continue your education. If you are young enough, and if there is no other way to fund your education, you may well decide to forgo some future retirement income now, with the hopes of more than making up for it in the future.

11
Locked-in Plans

There is nothing more frustrating than being in need of money and not being able to get at it, even though it legally belongs to you. Unfortunately, many people find themselves in exactly this situation every year. They have thousands of dollars invested in retirement accounts that they can't touch because the money is deemed to be "locked in." I've received correspondence from people saying they may have to declare bankruptcy as a result.

Locked-in plans normally result from the transfer of pension assets to a private account, for example, when you leave a company where you have contributed to their pension plan for several years. They are known by a variety of names, including Locked-in Retirement Account (LIRA), Life Income Fund (LIF), and Locked-in Retirement Income Fund (LRIF).

For many years, it was almost impossible to get money from these plans until the holder actually retired. Governments took the view that since the money originally came from a pension plan, it should be used for retirement income purposes and no other.

To their credit, some governments have been working to improve the situation in recent years. But because responsibility for pension administration is divided between

Ottawa and the provinces, we are stuck with a patchwork quilt of rules and regulations governing locked-in retirement money. Something that is allowed in one jurisdiction may be prohibited in another, and the rules governing the same type of plan may vary significantly.

To make matters worse, the ground keeps shifting. For example, a few years ago, just when residents of Ontario were finally figuring out the difference between a LIF and an LRIF, the provincial government reshuffled the deck by introducing a "new LIF," effectively tossing LRIFs and "old LIFs" into the dumpster—except for those who already had them and didn't take action to convert. More on this to follow.

Meantime, Ottawa and several provinces have been tinkering with the rules about "hardship" withdrawals from locked-in accounts, but everyone seems to have a different solution. No wonder people are confused!

The result is that if you want to withdraw money from a locked-in account, you need to know the rules that apply in your province. If your plan comes under federal authority (perhaps because the money came from a federal government pension plan), you'll need to check with the Office of the Superintendent of Financial Institutions (OSFI) by going to www.osfi-bsif.gc.ca/osfi/index_e.aspx?ArticleID=2660#1.

The federal rules for unlocking plans vary depending on age. At any age, you may apply to the financial institution that holds the plan (not directly to the federal government) to gain access to some or all of the money under the following conditions:

Financial hardship. This applies to people who are experiencing money problems due to low income or high medical/disability costs. For low-income people, the amount you may take out will depend on your expected cash flow for the year. If it is zero, you can withdraw up to 50 percent of the Year's Maximum Pensionable Earnings (YMPE), which was $51,100 in 2013. So a person with no income could take out $25,550. If your income is over 75 percent of the YMPE ($38,325 in 2013), no financial hardship withdrawal is allowed.

In the case of high medical bills, you can take out the amount of your expenditures up to a maximum of 50 percent of the YMPE, provided that the costs exceed 20 percent of expected annual income. The expenses can be incurred for you or for a dependant.

Non-residency. If you leave Canada for at least two years and are no longer employed by the company from which the pension money originated, you can apply to withdraw the full amount.

Shortened life expectancy. Anyone who is certified by a doctor to have shortened life expectancy, for example, due to a terminal illness, can apply to take all the money out of a locked-in plan.

People over age 55 have two additional withdrawal options under federal law:

One-time unlocking. This allows you to transfer up to 50 percent of the total amount in the plan into an unlocked registered plan, such as an RRSP or RRIF, from which you can then make ordinary withdrawals.

Small balance unlocking. You can take out the entire balance from your plan if your total locked-in holdings are below the minimum threshold, which is 50 percent of the YMPE. The funds may be withdrawn as cash, with the payment treated as income for tax purposes, or transferred to an RRSP or RRIF.

It is possible to use more than one option to get access to a larger amount of money. For example, if you use the one-time 50-percent unlocking option and the amount that remains in the plan meets the small balance requirements, then that option can be used, either in the same year or in any subsequent year.

Note that if you want to unlock funds under the financial hardship, one-time 50-percent, or small balance provisions, you will have to provide documentation that proves your spouse/partner agrees.

Those are the federal rules. But provincial differences also come into play. For example, in Ontario, the small balance option only applies if the amount in the plan is less than 40 percent of the YMPE, compared to 50 percent at the federal level. Ontario also has a provision that allows a surviving spouse/partner to transfer a survivor benefit directly to his/her own RRSP or RRIF. The governing body is the Financial

Services Commission of Ontario (FSCO), and you can find details at www.fsco.gov.on.ca/en/pensions/lockedin/faq/Pages/transferopt.aspx.

In British Columbia, it is much tougher to get money out of locked-in plans. There is no provision for financial hardship, and the small balance exception can only be used if the value of the plan is less than 20 percent of the YMPE. If you're age 65 or older, you can use the unlocking provision if the amount of money in the plan is less than 40 percent of the YMPE. The Financial Institutions Commission administers locked-in plans, and you can find details at www.fic.gov.bc.ca/pdf/Pensions/InformationForPlanMembers.pdf#Exceptions.

You'll find similar variations right across the country, so contact the provincial agency responsible for pension plan administration for details. This is a dog's breakfast of regulations, so take nothing for granted.

Early withdrawals are not the only point of confusion when it comes to locked-in plans. A few years ago, I received an email from a reader of my *Zoomer* magazine money column who was trying to figure out the options for his locked-in RRSP when he turned 71.

"It would be helpful to me and other Canadians if you could write an article on the subject, including a comparison of LIFs and LRIFs to highlight any differences, as well as their respective advantages and disadvantages," he wrote.

This is another example of confusing rules for locked-in plans. LIFs and LRIFs both have the same annual minimum withdrawal requirements as RRIFs, which are their unlocked equivalent. The difference is that there is no limit on the maximum amount of money that can be taken out of a RRIF in any given year. Both LIFs and LRIFs have maximum withdrawal ceilings, the idea presumably being to prevent people from raiding their retirement savings for frivolous reasons and being left penniless as a result.

The maximum annual withdrawal for a LIF is set by the jurisdiction that governs it. Let's look at the situation for a woman age 71 whose LIF was worth $100,000 on January 1, 2013. If her LIF came under federal jurisdiction, the maximum amount she could withdraw that year was $6415.30 (6.4153 percent). The full table can be found on the website of the Office of the Superintendent of Financial Institutions Canada at www.osfi-bsif.gc.ca/osfi/index_e.aspx?ArticleID=1560#q2.

However, if our pensioner's LIF was governed by the rules of Ontario, she would be allowed to withdraw up to $8454.80 (8.4548 percent) in 2013—more than $2000 in excess of what the feds allow. That table is available at www.fsco.gov.on.ca/en/pensions/policies/active/Documents/L200-412.pdf.

In British Columbia, the maximum annual LIF withdrawal varies according to the owner's age, current long-term interest rates, and the previous year's investment returns for the fund. In this case, our 71-year-old would be allowed to take out the greater of $8100 (8.1 percent) or the actual investment returns in the fund during 2012. So if her LIF gained 10 percent that year she could withdraw up to $10,000. You can read these details at www.fic.gov.bc.ca/index.aspx?p=pension_plans/life_income_fund_maximum_annual_withdrawal.

LRIFs, where they still exist, also impose an annual

maximum on the amount of money you can withdraw. However, the amount can be based either on the prescribed percentage for your age or, as with the B.C. LIF, on the profit generated by the plan in the previous year.

Do all these conflicting rules make any sense to you? Me neither!

But they keep coming. On January 1, 2010, Ontario introduced a new set of rules governing locked-in plans under its jurisdiction. These affected everyone who had an "old LIF," "new LIF," or LRIF that fell under the authority of the FSCO.

Under the amended regulations, "old LIF" and LRIF plan holders who switch their assets into a "new LIF" will have a one-time opportunity to apply to withdraw up to 50 percent of the plan's market value in cash or transfer the money to an RRSP or RRIF. This must be done within 60 days of converting to the "new LIF."

Although these changes were made a few years ago, many Ontarians are still not aware of them. However, there was no time limit, so you can still take advantage of them if you qualify.

Low-income people may wish to take their 50 percent in cash. The money will be taxable when it comes out of the plan, but the rate in these situations will be very low. Remember, you can withdraw "up to 50 percent," so you have flexibility in determining how much you will take out, thus enabling you to keep a lid on the tax bite. If all of the money is not needed immediately, make a maximum contribution to a TFSA. This will allow continued, tax-sheltered growth of the money and will eliminate all future tax on the profits earned.

People in higher tax brackets may prefer to do a direct tax-free transfer to an RRSP or RRIF. This removes any future maximum withdrawal impediments for that portion of the money.

Of course, if you have an "old LIF" or LRIF but you don't need any extra money right now, there is no need to take any action.

I have maintained for years that all this confusing regulation is anachronistic nonsense, a manifestation of paternalistic politics that may have been appropriate half a century ago but which is completely out of tune with 21st-century Canada. The money in locked-in accounts does not belong to governments; it belongs to individuals. Pension authorities should recognize that basic fact and remove all the red tape. Allow people to withdraw money as needed. No bureaucrat understands each personal situation better than the person involved.

12

RRSP or Mortgage Paydown?

Over the years, I have received many RRSP-related questions. The most frequent, by far, has been: "Should I make an RRSP contribution or pay down the mortgage?"

I wish there was an easy answer. There isn't. It depends on a number of variables as well as assumptions, some of which may be difficult to make at the time a decision is required.

Before getting into those variables, let's look at the pros and cons of each approach.

Making an RRSP Contribution

Pros. Putting money into a retirement plan allows you to build tax-sheltered capital to help finance your lifestyle once you stop work. The younger you are when you begin, the greater the effect of compounding over the years and the more money you'll have when you reach your desired retirement age. Conversely, the longer you wait to start contributing, the less money you will have.

Let's assume you want to retire at age 65. If you start contributing $5000 a year to an RRSP at age 25 and earn an average annual return of 6 percent, you will have accumulated over $820,000 by the time you stop work. However, if you wait until age 45 to begin because you have used the money to pay off the mortgage, your RRSP will be worth only $195,000 at retirement—less than one-quarter of the amount you would have had by starting earlier.

The other advantage of the RRSP contribution is the tax saving. You can claim a deduction for the amount contributed, and the higher your tax bracket, the more money that puts back in your pocket. For example, someone with a marginal tax rate of 25 percent will save $1250 on a $5000 RRSP contribution. But a person in a 45-percent bracket will have his/her tax reduced by $2250.

Cons. I assumed a 6 percent average annual return on the RRSP investments. But there is no guarantee you will actually earn that much, especially during periods of low interest rates. Any losses in the plan would reduce the end value, perhaps significantly. If the average annual return for our 25-year-old was only 3 percent, the final value would be about $388,000—less than half the total earned at 6 percent.

There is also the issue of taxes on withdrawals to consider. No matter how the money was earned inside the RRSP, all withdrawals are taxed at your marginal rate at that time. If it is higher than the rate that applied when the contribution was made, you'll end up a net loser on the deal.

Paying Down the Mortgage

Pros. You'll reduce your debt and own your home free and clear much sooner. In doing so, you'll save tens of thousands of dollars in interest costs. A $250,000 mortgage at 3.5 percent that is paid off over 25 years will cost you a whopping $124,152 in interest payments. By making additional payments of $5000 annually, the mortgage will be paid off after 18 years, and your total interest will be $80,303. That's a saving of almost $44,000.

You will also have the advantage of certainty, knowing that you'll reduce your interest cost each year by whatever rate you're paying. Your RRSP gains, by contrast, can only be estimated.

Cons. There is no tax deduction from a mortgage paydown. The money you use will come from after-tax dollars, which means you actually have to earn more in order to end up with enough cash for the payment. If you are in a 30-percent tax bracket, that means you need to earn about $7150 to have enough for a $5000 mortgage payment after the tax folks are finished with you.

Delaying the RRSP contribution to repay the mortgage will also result in a much-reduced retirement nest egg, as explained earlier.

Points to Consider

Clearly, this is not an easy decision. But here are some of the variables to consider that may help to clarify matters:

Tax brackets. The lower your tax bracket at the time of an RRSP contribution, the less financially advantageous your refund. By the same token, if you are in a low bracket, you will have to earn less money to make a mortgage payment because the government will be taking a smaller amount from your paycheque.

Your expected tax bracket in retirement is also relevant. In an analysis prepared for CIBC in February 2013, tax expert Jamie Golombek concluded that if your tax rate will be lower when it comes time to withdraw money from an RRSP or RRIF than it is today, the RRSP contribution is the better choice. The longer the money remains in the RRSP, the greater the benefit to you.

On the other hand, if you expect your tax rate to be higher in retirement than it is now, you'd be better off paying down the mortgage.

Rates of return. As mentioned, there is no certainty of the return you will earn in an RRSP, unless you invest exclusively in GICs. During periods of low interest rates, such a strategy would produce a minimal return.

However, if you have a fixed-rate mortgage, you'll know precisely how much you will be saving by making a lump-sum payment, in after-tax terms. For example, if the current term has four years to run and your interest rate is 4 percent, your annual saving on a $5000 prepayment is $200 after tax.

Pension plans. If you have a gilt-edged defined benefit pension plan, the decision becomes much easier: pay down the mortgage. You probably won't need an RRSP to help cover the cost of your retirement. It won't hurt to open one, of course—it's always nice to have too much money in retirement as opposed to not enough. But it's a luxury. In this case, a paid-off home is the better option.

Using a Calculator

Trying to work out an answer mathematically is a real challenge, but if you want to give it a try, you'll find a useful calculator at www.taxtips.ca/calculators/rrspvsmtgcalc.htm. However, be prepared to wade through a lot of numbers and what-if scenarios.

A note on the website pretty well sums up the conclusion: Unless your RRSP returns are going to be consistently higher than the rate on your mortgage, it is probably better to pay down your mortgage.

If you still can't make up your mind, try the old Canadian compromise: Make the RRSP contribution, and then use the refund to make a mortgage prepayment. That gives you the best of both worlds.

13
RRSP or Debt Paydown?

Deciding whether to make an RRSP contribution or pay down the mortgage can be a difficult decision, as we saw in the previous chapter. When it comes to other kinds of debt, however, the answer may be more clear-cut, especially in cases where the interest rate is exorbitant.

Credit cards are the most common example. A standard card charges an almost usurious 19.9 percent annually on unpaid balances. That's almost $20 on every $100 you carry, and that can take years to get rid of if you only make minimum payments.

How long? Here's a real example from my latest MasterCard bill. The total owing was $3357.82 with a minimum payment requirement of $70. On the last page of the statement, almost as an afterthought, was this reminder: "If you only make the minimum payment every month, it will take approximately 49 years and 10 months to pay off the entire new balance shown on this statement."

Yes, you read that correctly—almost half a century to discharge a debt of less than $3400. The interest cost of carrying that credit card debt will exceed the principal due many times over by the time you're finished.

And 19.9 percent isn't the highest rate—not by a long shot. If you have any department store–sponsored cards, check them out. A Hudson's Bay Company MasterCard will hit you for 29.9 percent on unpaid balances. The Sears MasterCard is the better choice at 19.9 percent, but that's still much too high.

I don't carry credit card balances—it's one of the worst financial mistakes anyone can make. But an estimated eight million Canadians do, and it's costing them a fortune.

Some of those people are making RRSP contributions. It's not often that I say this, but they should stop. This is a no-brainer.

Unless you have a low-interest card, the cost of carrying credit card debt will be far in excess of anything you could reasonably expect to earn in an RRSP. And the credit card interest is being paid in after-tax dollars, meaning you have to earn a whole lot more to have the cash to make even minimum payments.

It's far too easy to run up big credit card balances—card issuers are very liberal (arguably too liberal) in granting high credit limits. One of my cards has a limit of over $30,000, an amount I never requested and would never expect to use. It's much more difficult to pay off the balances, however, after they've accumulated.

That's where the money put aside for the RRSP contribution can make a big difference. Forget about the tax deduction for a year or two, and use the cash to bring the credit card balance to zero. Then cut up the card and switch to a debit card instead. That way you'll avoid repeating the mistake, and you can start building your RRSP without that cloud hanging over you.

What about other types of debt? That depends on the rate you are being charged and whether there are any tax breaks associated with it.

In the case of student loans, for example, an RRSP contribution is usually a better choice than an extra lump-sum payment. That's because the interest rates on these loans is very low—prime plus half a percent in Ontario, which has the country's largest student loan program. Also, the interest paid on these loans is tax-deductible, further reducing the true cost.

At the time of writing, the applicable rate on an Ontario student loan was 3.5 percent or $35 annually for every $1000 borrowed. Assuming the former student is now working and is in a 30-percent tax bracket, the after-tax cost is only $24.50 a year per $1000 borrowed.

Of course, anyone in this position should make the required annual loan repayment and not go into default, which would damage the credit rating. But any extra money should go into an RRSP, where it will generate a 30-percent tax deduction and earn tax-sheltered income for years to come.

Other types of loans, such as car loans and home equity lines of credit, should be assessed on the basis of the after-tax cost to you. Compare that to the combination of the RRSP deduction and the tax-sheltered compounding to decide which is the better course.

There are a number of loan repayment calculators available at www.fiscalagents.com/toolbox/index.shtml#tb4 that will help you to crunch the numbers. Make use of them.

14

RRSPs or TFSAs?

A few years ago, this wasn't even an issue. But since TFSAs were launched in 2009, many people now face an annual dilemma—which should they choose if they can only afford one?

There's no easy answer. TFSAs provide a valuable new option for retirement planning, but how they are best used will depend on each person's circumstances.

TFSAs and RRSPs are very different from a tax and savings perspective. In the jargon of economists, TFSAs are called TEE plans—taxed, exempt, exempt. That means the money going into the plan has already been taxed, but earnings within a TFSA are tax-exempt, as are all withdrawals.

In contrast, RRSPs are called EET plans—exempt, exempt, taxed. Contributions are tax-free because they generate an offsetting deduction. Investment income earned within an RRSP is also tax-free. But all the money that comes out is taxed at your marginal rate at that time, regardless of its source. That means you'll pay more tax on capital gains and dividends earned within an RRSP than you would if those same profits were generated in a non-registered account.

In the Budget Papers that explained the TFSA concept in

detail, the Department of Finance included an example that suggested there is no after-tax advantage in using either TFSAs or RRSPs for retirement savings. Based on their assumptions, both produced the same net after-tax return and both were equally superior to saving in a non-registered account. Here's the illustration they used.

Net Proceeds from Saving in a TFSA Relative to Other Savings Vehicles

	TFSA	RRSP	Unregistered savings
Pre-tax income	$1000	$1000	$1000
Tax (40% rate)	$ 400	–	$ 400
Net contribution[1]	$ 600	$1000	$ 600
Investment income (20 years at 5.5%)	$1151	$1918	$ 707[2]
Gross proceeds (Net contribution + investment income)	$1751	$2918	$1307
Tax (40% rate)	–	$1167	–
Net proceeds	$1751	$1751	$1307
Net annual after-tax rate of return[3] (%)	5.5	5.5	4.0

1. Forgone consumption (saving) is $600 in all cases. In the RRSP case, the person contributes $1000 but receives a $400 reduction in tax, thereby sacrificing net consumption of $600.
2. For the unregistered saving case, tax rate on investment income is 28%, representing a weighted average tax rate on an investment portfolio comprised of 30% dividends, 30% capital gains, and 40% interest.
3. Measured in relation to forgone consumption of $600. Assumes annual nominal pre-tax rate of return is 5.5% invested for 20 years.

This example assumes a contribution of $1000 to each of three different accounts—a TFSA, an RRSP, and an unregistered investment plan. But it is important to read the first footnote to the table to understand the rationale the Department of Finance used for the after-tax rate-of-return calculation. The figure is not based on the amount invested but rather on what Finance defines as "forgone consumption." This is the amount actually saved.

In all cases, the investor starts with a gross $1000. With the TFSA and the unregistered account, $400 is taken by taxes, leaving $600 in savings. That's straightforward enough, but the RRSP calculation is more complex: It appears at first glance that $1000 is the amount saved because that's what is paid into the plan and no tax is assessed because of the deduction generated. But the accepted way to make apples-to-apples comparisons in such situations is to examine it from the perspective of how much money a person could have spent if he or she had not made an investment. Using this approach, the "forgone consumption" is $600 in all cases. So the calculation of returns in all three scenarios is based on $600, although that number does not show up on the net contribution line in the RRSP column. For consistency, I'll stay with that approach in the analysis that follows.

Referring to the Finance table, you'll see that it shows the average annual compound rate of return for both a TFSA and an RRSP is 5.5 percent, and the tax rate going in and coming out is 40 percent. But if you change those basic assumptions, the end result can be quite different. Let's manipulate the numbers and consider the various outcomes. We'll begin by assuming that the contributor's marginal tax rate is lower in retirement than when he or she was working. We'll consider only a TFSA versus an RRSP because the results in an unregistered account don't change. Here is what happens, again using the "forgone consumption" of $600 as the base.

Net Proceeds from Saving in a TFSA Relative to an RRSP When the Final Tax Rate Is Lower

	TFSA	RRSP
Pre-tax income	$1000	$1000
Tax (40% rate)	$ 400	–
Net contribution[1]	$ 600	$1000
Investment income (20 years at 5.5%)	$1151	$1918
Gross proceeds (Net contribution + investment income)	$1751	$2918
Tax (30% rate)	–	$ 875
Net proceeds	$1751	$2043
Net annual after-tax rate of return (%)	5.5	6.3

1. Explanatory notes from the table on page 131 also apply here.

In this case, as the table shows, the RRSP is clearly the better choice. It produces an average annual compound rate of return of 6.3 percent over 20 years compared to 5.5 percent for a TFSA. This means that higher-income people who expect their tax rate to be lower after retirement should top up their RRSPs first before investing in a TFSA.

Now let's see what happens when the tax rate after retirement is higher than when a person was working.

Net Proceeds from Saving in a TFSA Relative to an RRSP When the Final Tax Rate Is Higher

	TFSA	RRSP
Pre-tax income	$1000	$1000
Tax (30% rate)	$ 300	–
Net contribution[1]	$ 700	$1000
Investment income (20 years at 5.5%)	$1342	$1918
Gross proceeds (Net contribution + investment income)	$2042	$2918
Tax (40% rate)	–	$1167
Net proceeds	$2042	$1751
Net annual after-tax rate of return (%)	5.5	4.7

1. Explanatory notes from the table on page 131 also apply here.

To sum up, if you expect your tax rate after retirement to be less than it is now, top up your RRSP before opening a TFSA. If you expect your tax rate after retirement to be higher than it is now, saving in a TFSA will produce a better return than making an RRSP contribution.

The C.D. Howe Analysis

In January 2010, the C.D. Howe Institute released a position paper by Alexandre Laurin and Finn Poschmann that examined the RRSP/TFSA issue in depth. One of its main conclusions was that even though TFSAs are not marketed as a retirement savings vehicle, for many people they are more tax-efficient than RRSPs "because the effective rate of tax payable on retirement income is often higher than that imposed on regular income during working life."

The study said that although most people expect their marginal tax rate will be lower after they retire, this is not necessarily the case. The authors acknowledged that it is easier for older workers to estimate their marginal effective tax rate (METR) after retirement than it is for young people with decades of saving time ahead of them, but found that some general rules can be applied.

"At low income levels, METRs at retirement significantly exceed those of working life," the report concluded. "This is caused mainly by the GIS clawback rate for seniors, which may be 50 or 75 percent depending on family configuration."

Somewhat surprisingly, they also concluded that where you live affects the decision on whether to use an RRSP or a TFSA for retirement saving.

"In Alberta in particular, where the tax system is less geared-to-income and simpler than in other provinces, individuals who are currently close to retirement appear better off putting their incremental retirement saving in a TFSA-like arrangement, rather than in a tax-deferred vehicle, no matter their target income-replacement rate," they wrote.

To address the situation, the authors recommended that the government give Canadians more flexibility to decide whether to allocate their retirement savings to TFSAs or RRSPs. One way to achieve this would be to combine the contribution limits for both programs and allow people to make their own allocations. As things stand right now,

RRSPs offer more contribution room to anyone whose earned income exceeds about $30,500.

Lower-Income Canadians

The C.D. Howe Institute has been highly critical of the way in which low-income savers are penalized by government policies when the time comes to draw on their RRSP or RRIF accounts. The most scathing denouncement was contained in Dr. Richard Shillington's 2003 paper, New Poverty Traps: Means Testing and Modest-Income Seniors.

"The primary beneficiary of this saving will be the federal and provincial governments because most of the income from it will be confiscated by income-tested programs and income taxes," Shillington wrote. "To the extent that these households have been misled, they have been defrauded."

The report makes a clear distinction between the value of RRSP saving for higher-income Canadians, who will ultimately benefit from their plans, and lower-income people, who will not. Dr. Shillington's message was that all those with less than $100,000 in retirement assets are "futile savers," because they will probably need financial support from governments after they stop work. Those benefits will be reduced or even eliminated if there is any income from RRSPs and RRIFs. (Remember: Every dollar in income from one of those plans reduces a GIS benefit by 50 cents once the $3500 exemption has been exceeded.)

Using a TFSA instead of an RRSP eliminates that problem, at least on the federal level. The federal government has ensured that TFSA withdrawals are not treated as income, nor will they be taken into account when calculating eligibility for GIS, tax credits, Employment Insurance, and so forth.

Clearly, anyone with a modest income should favour TFSAs over RRSPs for retirement savings purposes, even when the amounts being put aside are small.

No Earned Income

You cannot make an RRSP contribution unless you have what the government calls "earned income." Mostly, this is money earned from employment, but some other types of income, such as rents and alimony, also qualify. Investment income does not qualify as earned income, nor do pension payments, whether from the government or from a private plan.

If you don't have any earned income, or if the amount is small, TFSAs become your retirement savings vehicle by default. That's because you don't need any earned income to make a TFSA contribution.

Years ago, the typical Canadian family had one wage earner, usually the husband. The wife remained at home and raised the couple's children. Such families are less common today, but they still exist. In this situation, the wife is not able to save independently for her retirement through an RRSP because she has no earned income. If the wife has no earned income, the husband can make a spousal contribution on her behalf, but spousal RRSPs have significant restrictions on the ability to withdraw funds.

Now she has an option: a TFSA. She does not need to have

earned income to set up a personal retirement account. If she has some money of her own (perhaps from an inheritance from her parents), she can contribute some of it to the plan. Alternatively, she can use her husband's income to contribute, since income attribution rules will not apply in this case.

When RRSPs Are Better

There are some situations in which an RRSP is a better option than a TFSA—in fact, it may be the only choice. One example is a child or teenager with earned income. You must be 18 or older to open a TFSA, but there is no age limit for RRSPs. As long as a person has earned income, that person can have an RRSP account.

Most people don't realize this, so they pass up opportunities to encourage their children to put some of their earnings, however modest they may be, into an RRSP. For example, my granddaughter had a job at Canada's Wonderland, an amusement park north of Toronto, during the summer when she was 16. Her wages were modest, but they qualified as earned income for RRSP purposes. She was too young to open a TFSA, but she could contribute 18 percent of her earned income (the maximum allowed) to an RRSP. And she could defer claiming the tax deduction until she was working full-time, when the deduction will be more worthwhile. Meanwhile, the money will be compounding inside her RRSP.

She earned about $2800 over the summer. That allowed her to contribute $500 to an RRSP. At the time, she had 49 years before she would reach age 65. At an average annual growth rate of 5 percent, that $500 would grow more than 10 times, to $5460.67, at the end of that time. It's just one more example of the magic of compounding.

First-Time Homebuyers

One of the most popular features of RRSPs is the HBP. As discussed in chapter 9, this program allows first-time homebuyers to borrow up to $25,000 from an RRSP interest-free and to pay the money back over 15 years. Now aspiring homeowners face the dilemma of whether to use an RRSP or a TFSA as the savings vehicle for their down payment.

An RRSP allows you to reach your financial goal more quickly because you do not pay tax on RRSP contributions (you get an offsetting deduction), and your money therefore accumulates faster. Take a look at the following chart. It shows how much money would be accumulated in each plan based on $3500 a year in before-tax income. I've assumed an annual rate of return of 5 percent and, for purposes of the TFSA contributions, a marginal tax rate of 30 percent on the $3500.

Home Ownership Savings: RRSPs versus TFSAs

Year	RRSP	TFSA
1	$ 3675	$ 2573
2	$ 7534	$ 5274
3	$11,585	$ 8110
4	$15,840	$11,088
5	$20,307	$14,215
6	$24,997	$17,498

At the end of six years, you will have accumulated almost $25,000 in the RRSP and can take maximum advantage of the HBP. The value of the TFSA, however, is only $17,498 because you were only able to contribute $2450 a year after tax. It will be an additional two years before the TFSA reaches the $25,000 level, by which time you'll have your house.

If you had to withdraw the money outright from the RRSP to buy the home, it would be a different story, because the $25,000 would be taxed coming out. But with the HBP no tax is assessed on withdrawals as long as the loan is repaid on schedule or faster.

So, if saving for a first home is your number-one priority, the RRSP is the best way to do it. If you want to move even faster, use your RRSP refund to open a TFSA and save both ways.

Large Contributions

Because of the low contribution limits on TFSAs, big savers are better off using RRSPs because they can shelter more money from taxes. The maximum RRSP contribution for the 2014 tax year is $24,270, more than four times the amount you can put into a TFSA.

Of course, you're allowed to do both—the two types of plans can be used in tandem to build a supersized retirement nest egg.

Five Tests

If you are still unsure after reading this far, I've created five tests that you can apply to help you make up your mind. Here they are, with some background on each:

The age test. Everyone between 18 and 71 can ignore this one. For those who are still reading, the test is very simple. If you are over 71, a TFSA is your only choice. All RRSPs must be terminated, either by cashing out or converting to an income stream by December 31 of the year of your 71st birthday.

For those under 18, the RRSP is the only option because you can't open a TFSA until your 18th birthday. Most teens wouldn't even think about an RRSP, but if you have any earned income, perhaps from a summer job, you're eligible to contribute.

The pension test. Anyone with a blue-chip pension plan should opt for a TFSA. That's because they will have a secure income in retirement that will probably be above the national average. Withdrawals from an RRSP or RRIF, added to their pension, OAS, and CPP, could push these people into a high enough bracket that some or all of their OAS benefits will be clawed back. In 2013, the clawback kicked in when net income surpassed $70,954 (it is indexed to inflation so the amount increases annually). At that point, the tax rate for an OAS recipient is higher than that assessed on someone with a million-dollar income!

TFSA withdrawals are not considered to be income, so they will have no impact on the clawback.

The goals test. Ask yourself why you are saving. Is it for retirement? If so, the RRSP is generally the best choice because it has a much higher contribution limit. You can only put $5500 a year into a TFSA, but the RRSP limit is 18 percent of the previous year's earned income to a maximum of $24,270 in 2014.

If you are saving for a short-term goal, such as to buy a car, use a TFSA. If you put the money into an RRSP, it will be taxed coming out, perhaps at a higher rate than your contribution deduction was worth.

A TFSA is also the best choice for an emergency fund. If something unexpected happens, such as a job loss or critical illness, you'll want to be able to get at your money quickly, without having any held back for taxes.

For education savings, neither an RRSP nor a TFSA is the best choice. Instead, opt for an RESP where the federal government will also make a contribution of up to $500 a year on your behalf.

The support test. Do you expect to need government support, such as the Guaranteed Income Supplement (GIS), in your later years? Then choose the TFSA over the RRSP. As noted earlier, GIS payments and provincial support programs are income tested. If income exceeds $16,560, the GIS disappears completely.

RRSP withdrawals and RRIF payments count as income

for GIS calculations. This means that lower-income people who scrimped to put some money aside in an RRSP for retirement are penalized. You won't have that problem with TFSAs because the withdrawals are not considered as income for the GIS calculation.

The income test. Do you have any idea what your income is likely to be after retirement? If you do, it makes the TFSA/RRSP choice a lot easier. If your income will be lower than when you were working, go for the RRSP. Here's why. Let's say you're in a 35-percent tax bracket. For every $1000 you contribute to an RRSP, the government gives you back $350 as a tax refund. Your net cost is $650.

Let's assume that in retirement, your marginal tax rate will fall to 25 percent. You'll pay $250 in tax for every $1000 you withdraw from the plan. That's a good deal from a tax perspective.

It's the reverse if your income will be higher in retirement. For example, suppose your pension plan allows you to retire with full benefits after 30 years of service. You may decide to quit while you are still in your fifties and open a consulting business. With that income plus your pension you expect to make a lot more money than when you were an employee.

In this case, the TFSA is the better choice. The contributions will have been made with after-tax money when your marginal rate was 35 percent. But if you later move to a 40-percent rate, those tax-free withdrawals are going to look pretty attractive.

15
RRSP Mortgages

When you think about taking a mortgage on your property, the natural inclination is to go to a bank, credit union, or mortgage broker.

But there's another alternative—you can borrow the money from your RRSP, provided you have enough cash available and a self-directed plan. And the money won't be taxed when it comes out because, essentially, it's being invested in a debt security owned by the RRSP.

Most people are unaware of the RRSP mortgage option, but it is perfectly legal. The challenge is to find a financial institution that will agree to set it up for you—most won't.

It doesn't have to be a mortgage on your own home. You can use your RRSP money to help finance a home for a relative—perhaps a son or daughter just starting out—or even for an unknown third party.

However, the CRA has attached a number of strings to this seemingly generous concession whenever a mortgage is held in a retirement plan on a non-arm's-length basis— that is, a mortgage for a relative or yourself. You need to understand them before making any decision on whether an RRSP mortgage is a sensible choice.

Here are the basic rules that apply if you choose to use your RRSP as a non-arm's-length mortgage lender:

Market rates. The interest rate on a non-arm's-length RRSP mortgage cannot be less than the current rate being charged for a comparable term by a financial institution. In other words, your RRSP can't give you a break by charging a reduced rate of interest. However, since mortgage rates vary from one company to another, there is nothing to prevent you from choosing the lowest one you can find if your goal is to keep your payments low. Just be sure to retain evidence that the rate was in effect at the time the RRSP loan was incurred.

Insurance. Non-arm's-length RRSP mortgages must be administered by an approved lender under the National Housing Act (NHA) and must be insured, either through Canada Mortgage and Housing or a private company such as Genworth MI Canada. This rule applies even if the mortgage would normally not have to be insured if it were obtained through a financial institution.

Terms. The terms of the mortgage must be consistent with those normally available through commercial lenders. You're not allowed to give yourself the advantage of overly generous prepayment privileges, for example.

Default. An RRSP mortgage will be governed by all the conditions that apply normally, including the right of foreclosure. This means that if you default on your payments, your RRSP could end up owning your home—at least in theory. Of course, if you find yourself in that situation, your attitude might be: "Better my RRSP than the bank." Unfortunately, though, your RRSP can't hold real estate directly, so it would have to sell the house to another buyer at a reasonable price, normally within a year.

There are also considerations involved in holding your own mortgage that do not relate to Ottawa's rules:

Set-up costs. Starting one of these plans is pricey. You'll have to pay all the charges normally associated with applying for a mortgage, including appraisal costs, survey fees, and legal charges. On top of that, there's an initial set-up charge. This will vary depending on the financial institution with which you deal, but expect to pay in the range of $300. Mortgage insurance will be the single largest expense and is based on the amount of the loan. Get a quote and add up all the costs involved before proceeding.

Ongoing expenses. Here again, an RRSP mortgage will be more expensive than an ordinary conventional mortgage from a financial institution. Because an RRSP mortgage can only be held in a self-directed RRSP, you'll have to set up a plan and pay the annual administration fee associated with it. The basic cost of a self-directed plan can vary widely, but expect to pay between $100 and $150 a year. As well, a separate mortgage administration fee will be assessed. This will not be less than $100 and may run as high as $200.

Cash availability. You'll need to have enough cash in your RRSP to finance the mortgage. Your RRSP may have more than enough assets to make the payment, but they must be easily convertible to cash to do you any good. If the money is locked up in other investments, such as GICs, you won't have the necessary funds available. Because of the expenses involved, you should have access to at least $100,000 in your RRSP to consider this idea.

Personal cash flow. You need to make regular payments to the plan, just as you would with a regular mortgage. Make sure your budget can handle it.

Reinvesting interest payments. The borrower will be making regular mortgage payments to your RRSP, probably on a monthly basis. If these are relatively small—say, a few hundred dollars each month—you may have trouble reinvesting the money immediately. Most GICs, for example, have a $1000 minimum. Therefore, it may be necessary to let your mortgage payments accumulate for several months before reinvesting them. Since interest paid on cash balances is normally very low, this can have the effect of reducing returns.

Lack of flexibility. Once you've set up the mortgage, your money is locked in. You can't easily shift it somewhere else to take advantage of new investment opportunities that may arise.

Given all these negatives, why would anyone consider holding a mortgage in their RRSP? Actually, there are several possible reasons.

First, you're paying mortgage interest to yourself, not to a financial institution. Sure, it costs the same amount of money, but some people derive a lot of satisfaction from knowing that it's being paid to their retirement fund and not padding a bank's bottom line.

Second, you may be able to use an RRSP mortgage to help out a child who might otherwise have difficulty financing a home.

Third, you may want some cash for home renovations but would prefer not to work with a bank or credit union. An RRSP mortgage could provide the money you need.

Fourth, if you're uncertain about your investing skills, an RRSP mortgage is a way to ensure a steady rate of return for your retirement plan—assuming, of course, that all payments are made on time. Even in times of low interest rates, mortgage rates are usually two to three percentage points higher than those offered on a GIC of comparable term. For example, at the time of writing, Royal Bank was offering only 2.2 percent on a five-year non-redeemable GIC whereas their posted mortgage rate for the same term was 5.14 percent.

Over many years, that extra income would appear to boost the value of your RRSP considerably. However, you have to factor in the costs of the RRSP mortgage to be sure you are in fact going to end up better off. To make a profit, you have to earn enough additional interest on your mortgage each year to offset the higher administration costs and the extra burden of paying off the insurance premium, which is tacked on to your mortgage principal. Of course, if you don't care about the profit side, perhaps because the loan was made to help one of your children, that won't matter.

Another option to consider if you want to maximize the return on an RRSP mortgage is to find an unrelated person who is looking for a loan and is willing to pay above-market rates. There is nothing in the rules that says the loan must be for a first mortgage. Here are a couple of examples of how to use this option:

A second or third mortgage at a premium rate. A mortgage broker or lawyer who specializes in the field may be able to find you a quality second or third mortgage that offers a much better return than you can obtain from other types of fixed-income securities. Normally, the risk on these mortgages is higher, but you may be able to find one that is fully secured by equity in the property and/or where the borrower has impeccable credit credentials. Typically, mortgages of this type will have a relatively short term, perhaps two or three years. The interest rate you receive should be at least three percentage points higher than the going market rate on first mortgages.

A vendor take-back mortgage. If you're trying to sell your house, an attractive sweetener can be a vendor take-back mortgage. This simply means you assume some or all of the mortgage loan. If you don't want to tie up your own cash, a mortgage of this type could be placed in your RRSP.

There are fewer restrictions on arm's length mortgages, an important one being that they do not have to be insured. The CRA's only stipulation is that the mortgaged property be located in Canada.

Third-party borrowers can usually be found through a mortgage broker. A few companies actively encourage this business, such as Canadian Western Trust and B2B Bank. The latter company even makes arrangements for drawing funds from a combination of accounts to finance large mortgages.

Interest in RRSP mortgages tends to be much greater when rates are high. However, as we have seen, these plans offer a respectable spread between GIC rates and mortgage rates even during low-interest periods.

If you have enough cash in an RRSP, it's an option worth considering. Just be sure to crunch all the numbers first to make sure it's cost-effective.

16
Having It Both Ways

There is nothing mutually exclusive about TFSAs and RRSPs. You can use the two in combination to tax shelter almost all of your invested money. In fact, Finance Minister Jim Flaherty, the godfather of TFSAs, said after the bill was introduced in 2008 that the day may come when 90 percent of Canadian personal investments are protected from direct taxation by using the two programs in combination. We can already see that pattern taking shape as the amount of money that can be held in TFSAs increases each year. In 2015, for example, a couple who were both 18 or over in 2009 and residents of Canada will have $73,000 worth of TFSA contribution room between them.

The loss of tax revenue on investment income will be substantial, and future finance ministers will have to figure out how to deal with that problem. But it's doubtful that one of the solutions will be to drastically change the RRSP or TFSA rules, as some people fear. Once programs such as these become established, it becomes almost politically impossible to withdraw them or even radically amend them.

The result is that Canada offers an opportunity to tax-shelter savings that is almost unique in the world. All you have to do is take advantage of it by using RRSPs and TFSAs in smart combinations. Here are three ideas:

Shelter RRIF withdrawals. At age 71, RRSPs must be wound up. In most cases, the money is transferred to a RRIF. At this point, the government requires you to withdraw a certain amount of money each year and to pay taxes on it. The actual amount will be based on your age at the time and the amount of money in the plan on January 1 of the year in question.

In some cases, people need the entire amount of the withdrawal to live on. But sometimes not all the RRIF funds are required, perhaps because the person has a healthy pension plan or a frugal lifestyle. The tax still has to be paid on the withdrawal, but some or all of the after-tax amount can then be deposited to a TFSA, thereby sheltering future investment income from all taxes. Over a few years, this can add up to a lot of money.

Here's an example. Let's use a RRIF with a value of $250,000 on January 1. The annuitant, we'll call him Stan, is 72 years old. The federal government formula requires that a minimum of 7.48 percent, or $18,700, be withdrawn from the plan that year. Stan is in a 30-percent bracket so he's left with $13,090 after tax. He only needs $6000 of that to live on because he has income from other sources, including the CPP and OAS. That leaves $7090. He puts $5500 of that into his personal TFSA and gives the rest to his wife to deposit into her own plan. Now that money can be reinvested, and neither of them will ever have to pay any tax on the income or the amount they contributed.

Project this out over five years, assuming a 5 percent investment return in each plan and assuming the numbers stay constant (they won't, but this is just an illustration). At that point, Stan's TFSA will be worth almost $32,000 while his wife will have another $9200 in her plan. That's more than $41,000 between them, all tax exempt!

Deposit RRSP refunds in a TFSA. One of the big attractions of RRSPs is the tax refund they generate. Unfortunately, many people take that money and run—they don't think about reinvesting it to increase their tax-sheltered net worth. In doing so, they are missing out on a great opportunity.

Using an RRSP refund to build a TFSA gives you the best of both worlds—a tax-sheltered retirement plan and a tax-exempt investment account that can be used for any purpose you want.

Let's look at the math. Joanne makes a $10,000 RRSP contribution. She is in a 35-percent tax bracket so her refund is $3500. If she spends that money and the RRSP grows at an annual rate of 5 percent, the original $10,000 will be worth about $16,300 after 10 years.

But suppose she uses the $3500 to open a TFSA, which also earns 5 percent. After 10 years, the combined value of the two plans will be almost $22,000—an improvement of 35 percent. And that's just based on a single year.

If Joanne repeated the process every year for a decade, the RRSP would grow to $132,000 while the TFSA would be worth over $46,000, for a total of more than $178,000. After 20 years, the combined value would be almost $469,000. We're talking big money here!

Draw down RRSPs. Normally, I would not advise taking money out of an RRSP to contribute to a TFSA, but there are times when such a strategy would make sense. Usually, this occurs when the RRSP holder experiences one or more years of low income, thereby minimizing or even negating the tax on an RRSP withdrawal.

One example would be a woman who takes time away from her career to have a family. Let's say that Ada has worked for 10 years as a graphic artist, earning a good salary and contributing regularly to an RRSP. She becomes pregnant and decides to take two years off to raise the child. Her husband earns enough to make this possible.

Over those two years, Ada's earned income will be zero. This means she could withdraw money tax-free from her RRSP and move it to a TFSA, as long as she does not exceed the federal basic personal amount, which was $11,038 for the 2013 tax year (it increases annually because of indexing).

This strategy is not entirely without tax consequences, however. For starters, there will be withholding tax on her RRSP withdrawals, although this can be recovered when she files her tax return. More important is the fact that her husband's ability to claim a spousal tax credit will be reduced by the amount Ada withdraws from the RRSP, thereby increasing his tax bill. If she takes out $5000, his federal tax will increase by 15 percent of that, or $750. However, they may decide that's a worthwhile price to pay to ensure that the money is not taxed at a much higher rate when Ada eventually retires and begins to receive RRIF payments.

The RRSP drawdown/TFSA contribution strategy makes sense for people who are reasonably sure their current tax bracket is lower than it will be once they have to begin taking RRIF withdrawals. But do the math before you take any action.

17
Cutting Your Tax Bill

Everyone knows that an RRSP contribution generates a tax deduction. However, there's a lot more to it than that when it comes to taxation and your retirement plan. There are other ways to use your RRSP to reduce the amount of money you have to pay governments. And there are some rules you need to know so as not to run into unexpected tax hits. Here are eight helpful tax-saving tips:

Tip #1: Open a Spousal Plan

Setting up a spousal RRSP will allow you to split income with your spouse or partner after retirement—something that may or may not be financially beneficial, depending on your circumstances. It can also be a useful strategy in specific situations, such as when one spouse has a much lower income.

A spousal RRSP does not increase your contribution entitlement, and there are restrictions on withdrawing money from the plan. So the main benefit is a long-range one: It sets the stage for income splitting during your retirement years. That's because any income from an annuity or RRIF purchased with funds from a spousal RRSP will be considered your spouse's for tax purposes. That's often—but not always—a desirable objective. The problem is trying to figure out whether setting up a spousal RRSP will work for or against you 15 or 20 years from now.

The introduction of pension income splitting has diminished the popularity of spousal plans in recent years. However, there are still circumstances in which they can be useful.

Income splitting in retirement can save hundreds or even thousands of dollars in taxes. For example, a British Columbia resident with taxable income of $50,000, all from pensions and RRIFs, was taxed at a top rate of 29.7 percent for the 2013 tax year. But if that income was split 50–50 between two spouses, each would have a marginal tax rate of 23.26 percent. According to Ernst & Young's online tax calculator, the tax on $50,000 paid to one person would have been $8633. But splitting the income between spouses results in a total tax bill of $5296, a saving of $3337. That's a lot of money on a $50,000 income.

The advantage of a spousal RRSP in creating this scenario is that it provides more flexibility. The rules governing pension income splitting are very strict. For example, withdrawals from an RRSP are not eligible; you would have to convert the plan to a RRIF to qualify, and then only after age 65, except in the case of the death of a spouse.

A spousal RRSP enables a lower-income husband or wife to withdraw money at any time (subject to the restrictions outlined below) as needed. This allows conversion to a RRIF, and the forced withdrawals that come with such a move, to be delayed until age 71.

Another benefit from a spousal RRSP (and from pension income splitting) may be to avoid the clawback of OAS payments. For 2013, the clawback tax was 15 percent of net income in excess of $70,954, or the full amount of your OAS payment, whichever is less. The threshold applies to each individual. So if one spouse has taxable income of $100,000, he or she will have most of the OAS payment taxed back. But if income is split, each spouse can receive up to $70,954 (or almost $142,000 between them) and avoid the clawback. The threshold is indexed to inflation so will increase each year.

A third potential advantage of a spousal plan relates to the age credit that is available to anyone age 65 and up. However, this credit is subject to an income test. It works like this. You're allowed to receive net income up to $34,562 (2013 figures) and still qualify for the full credit. If your income is higher, a special calculation comes into play. This begins with the "age amount"—the figure used for calculating the age credit. For the 2013 tax year, it was $6854. The actual tax credit—the amount you can deduct from your federal tax payable—is 15 percent of the age amount, or $1028.10.

If your net income exceeds the threshold, you'll have to multiply the excess amount by 15 percent. The result is subtracted from the age amount. You then multiply the revised age amount figure by 15 percent to arrive at the allowable age tax credit.

To illustrate, suppose your net income was $40,000 in 2013. That's $5438 over the limit. Here's what happens:

$$\$5438 \times 15\% = \$815.70$$
$$\$6854 - \$815.70 = \$6038.30$$
$$\text{Age credit} = \$6038.30 \times 15\% = \$905.75$$

In this case, you've lost $122.35 of your federal tax credit. When provincial taxes are factored in, the result will be a tax bill that's about $175 more than it would have been.

A spousal RRSP might enable a couple to bring both of their incomes to below the threshold, thus preserving the full tax credit for each of them.

Here's another example of how a spousal RRSP can be useful. Let's consider a couple in which one spouse (we'll say the wife) has no income while the other has a full-time job. The husband opened a spousal RRSP several years ago and contributed to it regularly.

They now find themselves in financial difficulty—perhaps the house needs extensive repairs. They need some extra money quickly. Because the wife has no income, she can tap into her spousal plan to get the needed money. The husband will lose some of his spousal tax credit when she does this, but as long as she does not take out more than about $11,000, she won't have to pay any tax on the withdrawal (the withholding tax will be refunded when she files her return). But check out the withdrawal restrictions before doing this.

There are situations when a spousal RRSP can actually end up costing you money. Higher-income families need to be especially careful.

Let's go back to the OAS clawback again. This time, let's consider two married professionals. Let's say the wife is a partner in a law firm and is projected to have an income of $150,000 a year in retirement. The husband is a school principal and expects retirement income of $70,000. The wife will lose the entire OAS benefit, but the husband won't be hit by the clawback.

If the wife set up a spousal RRSP to shift income to her husband, the story would be quite different, however. Let's say she managed to move $20,000 worth of income into his hands in this way. She would still have all her OAS benefit clawed back. But now he'd also be on the hook, and would stand to lose a portion of his OAS payments.

So a spousal plan can be a benefit, or a trap. For most people, however, it will usually work out to their advantage.

The one area you have to be careful about is withdrawals. You cannot take funds out of a spousal plan within three years of making a contribution. If you contributed to a spousal RRSP in 2012, 2013, or 2014, and any funds were withdrawn by either you or your spouse or the plan was collapsed in 2014, you may have a tax problem. You'll normally have to declare the amount of your contributions to the plan during those three years as income on your 2014 return.

However, if the withdrawal is less than your contributions, you can declare the smaller amount. For example, suppose you contributed $3000 a year to a spousal plan in each of 2012, 2013, and 2014, and claimed tax deductions totalling $9000 over the period. Late in 2014, your spouse withdraws $10,000 from the plan. You (not your spouse) would have to pay tax on your $9000 worth of contributions in the 2014 tax year. But if your spouse only withdrew $5000, your tax liability would be for that amount.

If the withdrawal is made as part of the HBP or LLP, these attribution rules do not apply.

Converting the RRSP to a RRIF changes the situation somewhat. If you contributed to any spousal RRSP during the past three years, your spouse/partner may withdraw the legal minimum amount from a spousal RRIF without penalty. But any additional funds withdrawn will be attributed back to you for tax purposes.

Tip #2: Defer Claiming Deductions

You do not have to claim a tax deduction for the year in which you make an RRSP contribution. You can effectively bank it until such time as it will be of maximum benefit to you.

Take the case of a recent college graduate who is just beginning a career with a brokerage firm. Her starting salary is $35,000 a year and she lives in Saskatchewan. She knows the importance of starting an RRSP early so she sets up an automatic monthly plan to deduct $250 from her salary, or $3000 for the year. She is in a 26-percent tax bracket, so if she claimed the deduction immediately, it would be worth $780.

However, within six months she receives a promotion and is told by her employer that her prospects for advancement are very good. She can reasonably expect to be earning at least $50,000 within two years. At that point, her marginal rate would be up to 35 percent and that $3000 contribution would save her $1050 in tax, or $270 more than if she had claimed it immediately.

There's always a temptation to grab any tax savings immediately. But if you have reason to believe that you'll be in a higher tax bracket within a few years, being patient can pay off in a big way.

Tip #3: Make Opportunistic Withdrawals

There may be times in life when you can take money out of your RRSP with little or no tax consequence. These typically arise when the contributor or a spouse leaves the workforce for a while, perhaps to raise a family or due to illness. With income reduced to zero, it's possible to withdraw about $11,000 (the basic personal amount) from an RRSP without incurring tax (although be sure to look at the effect on a spouse/partner because of the loss of the spousal credit).

This is not to suggest that it's a good idea to pull money out of your plan for the sake of doing so. Any withdrawals will reduce the amount of tax-sheltered income you can earn and compromise your retirement income down the road. But if the money is badly needed or you want to move it into a TFSA, this strategy can make sense.

Tip #4: Be Wary of Foreign Withholdings

Under the Canada–U.S. Tax Treaty, dividends and interest from American corporations that are paid to your RRSP are not taxed. (There is a withholding tax of 15 percent on U.S. dividends paid to non-registered accounts and TFSAs.)

However, you may be hit with withholding tax on dividends and distributions from other types of foreign securities. For example, American Depositary Receipts (ADRs), which trade on U.S. exchanges, are proxies for major foreign companies such as Unilever, Sony, and Air France. Although you may buy shares for your RRSP on the New York Stock Exchange, ADRs are not protected by the tax treaty and may be subject to withholding tax of as much as 35 percent on dividends. Worse, there is no way to recover that money because the dividend was paid to a tax-sheltered retirement account.

Payments from certain types of U.S. securities also fall outside the ambit of the tax treaty. Limited partnerships are an example—they are not only subject to a high withholding tax of 35 percent but you could also end up having to file a U.S. tax return by owning them. They should be avoided at all costs, tempting though their yields may be.

I recommend that you ask your financial adviser or an accountant about the tax implications of buying any foreign securities for your RRSP that are not publicly traded shares in U.S. corporations.

Tip #5: Make Your Portfolios Tax-Efficient

If you are fortunate enough to have a non-registered investment portfolio as well as an RRSP, make sure that it is set up in the most tax-effective way. This means holding the securities that attract the highest rate of taxation (interest income) in the RRSP, while keeping tax-advantaged investments (like dividend-paying stocks) in the non-registered portfolio.

Begin the process by reviewing the total amount of money invested in both portfolios. Decide what percentage you want to hold in fixed-income securities such as bonds, bond funds, and GICs. Those assets should go into the RRSP. Put the stocks, mutual funds, REITs, etc. in the non-registered portfolio, which will enable you to take advantage of the dividend tax credit and the 50-percent exemption on capital gains.

If your RRSP is quite large and the non-registered portfolio is small, it may be necessary to put some of the growth securities into the registered plan to achieve your target asset mix.

Don't make the mistake of mirroring the two portfolios. A few years ago an investment advisory firm did exactly that with the account of a friend. It was costing her about $2000 a year in unnecessary taxes until I pointed it out. Needless to say, she fired the company.

Tip #6: Repay HBP, LLP Loans

There is no legal obligation to repay RRSP loans under the Home Buyers' Plan and Lifelong Learning Plan. But if you don't, the amount owing will be added to your income in the year it is due and taxed accordingly. If your income has gone up in the interim, you could end up paying tax on that money at a higher rate than the value of the refund you received at the time of the contribution. Plus your RRSP will lose out on the tax-sheltered income the repayment money could have generated.

Tip #7: Avoid Overcontributions

As I explained in chapter 8, you can carry a lifetime overcontribution of up to $2000 in an RRSP. However, if you get beyond that, the CRA will slap you with a penalty of 1 percent monthly on the excess. That can get very costly over time.

Tip #8: Understand the Withholding Rules

When you make an RRSP withdrawal, the financial institution is required to withhold a certain amount for taxes. The percentage depends on the amount withdrawn and whether you live in Quebec or the rest of Canada. Here is the table.

Amount withdrawn	Quebec	Rest of Canada
Up to $5000	5%	10%
$5001–$15,000	10%	20%
Over $15,000	15%	30%

At first glance it looks as if Quebecers get a break, but that's not the case. The provincial tax is added to the rest-of-Canada percentage, resulting in a higher withholding in Quebec than elsewhere.

Many people mistakenly believe that these are the actual tax rates that apply to RRSP withdrawals. They are not. This is just a prepayment, similar to the amount withheld from every paycheque. The actual amount of tax you pay on an RRSP withdrawal will be determined when you file your tax return for the year since any money taken out of the plan will be treated as ordinary income.

For example, you withdraw $5000 from an RRSP and have $500 withheld. But when you file your return, your income (which now includes that $5000) puts you in a 30-percent tax bracket. That brings the total tax bill on the withdrawal to $1500, and you'll be assessed an additional $1000 on your return ($1500 less the $500 already withheld).

Be sure to take this into account when you're considering making an RRSP withdrawal, otherwise you could be in for an unpleasant surprise at tax time.

18
Death and Taxes

There seems to be a lot of confusion about exactly what happens to the money in RRSPs, RRIFs, TFSAs, and other registered plans when you die. The following question from a reader is typical of the ones I receive regularly: "Is it true that upon my demise, my daughters will be taxed if they cash in my RRSP, TFSA, and investment portfolio? They are my beneficiaries in my will. Would that be like a death tax? Also, if they have their own RRSP accounts, could they transfer my funds without having to pay taxes?"

There are several issues to be addressed here, but let me start with one very basic point: If you have a living spouse/partner, there is no need for concern. The government won't take a penny of your money—providing you get the paperwork right.

In the case of retirement plans such as a RRIF, RRSP, or LIF, designate your spouse as the beneficiary. Ideally, this should have been done when the plan was opened, but it is never too late. Just contact the plan administrator and ask for the appropriate forms. If both spouses have retirement plans, each should name the other as beneficiary.

By doing this, you ensure that all the assets in your plan are transferred directly into an RRSP/RRIF owned by the surviving spouse. There are no taxes of any kind on this transfer.

Failure to make a beneficiary designation means the assets will go to your estate by default. That means they may be subject to probate, which can be expensive and time-consuming.

The same rules apply if you have a dependent child or grandchild.

Although this book deals with RRSPs, it's worthwhile comparing the tax treatment of retirement plans with the procedure for TFSAs. For these plans, you want to designate your spouse as the "successor holder" unless you live in Quebec, in which case you must use the beneficiary designation. (The rules of succession are a provincial responsibility, which is why this gets so complex.)

The successor holder can only be the spouse or common-law partner of the person who owns the TFSA. (Common-law partners must have lived together for at least three years or have children together.) No one else qualifies. The successor holder takes control of the TFSA when the original account holder dies. No taxes are payable.

However, successor holders do not inherit any unused contribution room from the deceased. Any new contributions will be deducted from their personal limit. The successor holder can also make a new beneficiary designation and may cash out the plan at any time, tax-free.

Many TFSA investors have not named a successor holder because they weren't offered the option when the plan was set up. At the time TFSAs were launched, in January 2009, only a few provinces had passed legislation to allow successor holders to be named (and not by that specific term). The rest dragged their heels, in some cases until mid-year. The result was widespread uncertainty. Residents of some provinces (British Columbia, Alberta, Nova Scotia, New Brunswick, and Prince Edward Island) were allowed to make successor holder designations as part of their TFSA application. But in the rest of the country, including populous Ontario, they were not.

The practical effect of this provincial tardiness is that anyone who was unable to name a successor holder when they opened an account must now go back to the plan administrator and complete the required form. I strongly advise doing this since it will make the whole transfer process much easier if anything should happen to you. Anyone opening a new account should be able to do this without difficulty.

But suppose you have no spouse or dependent children/ grandchildren. Then what? The rules are very different depending on whether you're dealing with a TFSA or a registered retirement plan.

For a TFSA, you need to name a beneficiary. That can be anyone you wish: a child, sibling, relative, friend, or charity. The beneficiary will receive the assets of a TFSA, tax-free, at death, and the plan will be terminated. However, any profits earned within the TFSA between the time the holder dies and the date it is wound up will be taxable in the hands of the beneficiary.

This means that the full value of the TFSA at the time of death will pass to your heir with no tax, which makes these plans a valuable estate planning tool.

(Warning: Don't name your spouse and someone else as joint beneficiaries. If you do, the rules of the game change; the transfer of assets will become more complicated because the spouse will no longer qualify as a successor holder.)

Now let's look at RRSPs/RRIFs. This is where governments collect their pound of flesh. Going back to the question at the beginning of this chapter, technically our reader's daughters won't pay any tax on the RRSP assets. But before the assets are conveyed to the beneficiaries, the estate will. The net result is that the daughters will get less.

RRSPs are deemed to be cashed out when you die (RRIFs and LIFs are treated the same). The assets in the plan will form part of your income on your final tax return (the one that will be filed by your executor after you die), and will then be taxed at your marginal rate.

Obviously, the more money that is in the RRSP/RRIF, the higher the tax. However, the widely held belief that the government will take half of a plan's value is, in most cases, not correct. Only top-bracket residents of Nova Scotia are hit with a 50-percent marginal tax rate, although Quebec comes very close at 49.97 percent. In other provinces, the maximum (based on 2013 rates) ranges from a low of 39 percent (Alberta) to a high of 47.37 percent (PEI). So one way to cut taxes on your retirement plans is to move to Alberta.

The reader also asked if she could transfer RRSP assets into her daughters' accounts. The answer is no—that is prohibited by law. However, she could give them gifts of money from a non-registered account with no tax implications, assuming they are adults. Also, if she is in a low tax bracket, it might be worthwhile making relatively small annual withdrawals, paying the tax, and then gifting the balance to the daughters.

As you can see, this can be something of a minefield, so let me sum it up in a few sentences:

1. Name your spouse/partner as the successor holder of your TFSA.
2. If you have no spouse, designate a TFSA beneficiary.
3. Name your spouse/partner as the beneficiary of your RRSP/RRIF.
4. If you have no spouse, name someone else as beneficiary and consider tax-reduction strategies to minimize the hit to your RRSP/RRIF when you die.
5. Sign all the appropriate papers now—don't put it off.

19
The Wealth-Building Machine

Although RRSPs have become one of our most important savings vehicles, many people have no idea just how much wealth can be built, over the years, in a retirement plan.

In fact, an RRSP is the closest thing to a personal money machine any of us will ever have. If you start early enough and make regular contributions, there's an excellent chance your plan will be worth upwards of $100,000 and perhaps even more than $1 million by the time you're 65. And, if you invest wisely, the total could be a great deal more!

It may be hard to believe that you can accumulate so much money, but it's true. There are three key ingredients in making it happen: regular contributions, the magic of compounding returns, and the tax-sheltered environment of an RRSP.

Consider the following examples of RRSP growth. I've selected the contribution limits to reflect three types of situations.

A target contribution for many people with relatively low incomes is $1200 a year ($100 a month). The allowable deduction for someone with $40,000 earned income and no pension plan is $7200 a year. The maximum contribution for a non–pension plan member for the 2014 tax year is $24,270.

You need earned income of about $135,000 to qualify for this amount.

I've assumed in all cases that funds within the plan earn 6 percent each year, compounded annually, that the contributions were made at the start of the year, and that the return was paid at year-end (of course, this won't always be the case; this is just an illustration). Note that 6 percent won't be attainable unless you diversify your RRSP by using mutual funds or other investments with growth potential, such as stocks.

$1200 Annual Contribution and 6 Percent Rate of Return

Number of years	Total invested	Value at retirement
10	$12,000	$ 16,766
15	$18,000	$ 29,607
20	$24,000	$ 46.791
25	$30,000	$ 69,788
30	$36,000	$100,562
35	$42,000	$141,745
40	$48,000	$196,857

$7200 Annual Contribution and 6 Percent Rate of Return

Number of years	Total invested	Value at retirement
10	$ 72,000	$ 100,596
15	$108,000	$ 177,642
20	$144,000	$ 280,748
25	$180,000	$ 418,726
30	$216,000	$ 603,372
35	$252,000	$ 850,470
40	$288,000	$1,181,143

$24,270 Annual Contribution and 6 Percent Rate of Return

Number of years	Total invested	Value at retirement
10	$242,700	$ 339,092
15	$364,050	$ 598,802
20	$485,400	$ 946,353
25	$606,750	$1,411,455
30	$728,100	$2,033,867
35	$849,750	$2,866,793
40	$970,800	$3,981,437

If you look at the above tables closely, two things become obvious immediately:

1. The greatest growth takes place in the later years. So the longer you wait to begin, the less your RRSP will be worth when you retire. In fact, if you begin contributions in your early 20s and stop when you reach age 35, leaving the balance in your RRSP, you'll end up with more money at 65 than if you waited until you were 35 to begin and contributed every year thereafter.

2. The amount of your annual contribution has a significant effect on the ultimate value of your RRSP. After 40 years, the end value of an RRSP to which $7200 is contributed annually is almost $1 million more than one to which $1200 is contributed annually—even though the difference in the total amount contributed over that time is only $240,000.

The other important factor that will determine the final amount in your RRSP is your rate of return. The above tables were calculated on the basis of a 6 percent annual return. The next set of tables is based on 8 percent. That means taking on somewhat more risk, but it is not an impossible goal. Check out the differences.

$1200 Annual Contribution and 8 Percent Rate of Return

Number of years	Total invested	Value at retirement
10	$12,000	$ 18,775
15	$18,000	$ 35,189
20	$24,000	$ 59,308
25	$30,000	$ 94,745
30	$36,000	$146,815
35	$42,000	$223,323
40	$48,000	$335,737

$7200 Annual Contribution and 8 Percent Rate of Return

Number of years	Total invested	Value at retirement
10	$ 72,000	$ 112,648
15	$108,000	$ 211,135
20	$144,000	$ 355,845
25	$180,000	$ 568,472
30	$216,000	$ 880,890
35	$252,000	$1,339,935
40	$288,000	$2,014,423

$24,270 Annual Contribution and 8 Percent Rate of Return

Number of years	Total invested	Value at retirement
10	$242,700	$ 379,716
15	$364,050	$ 711,700
20	$485,400	$1,199,494
25	$606,750	$1,916,224
30	$728,100	$2,969,334
35	$849,750	$4,516,699
40	$970,800	$6,790,286

The impact of those additional two percentage points of return each year can be seen clearly by looking at the value of the RRSP after 40 years in which the annual contribution is $7,200. At retirement, the plan that earned 8 percent annually has almost $1 million more than the one that earned 6 percent! Remember, nothing else changed—only the annual return on the invested money.

In the case of the $24,270 annual contribution, the difference after 40 years is about $2.8 million! Of course, you have to be in a top income bracket to contribute that much money to an RRSP, but the table dramatically illustrates why it's so important to manage your RRSP funds effectively.

If you want to estimate how much your own RRSP will be worth when you retire, you can use the following table. Choose how many years down the road and what rate of return you're looking at. Where those two intersect in the table gives you the multiplication factor you use with your anticipated annual contribution. In each case, we've assumed that your contribution is made at the start of the year and that interest is compounded annually and paid at the end of each year. The percentages are the projected average annual compound rate of return.

Future Value of Regular RRSP Contributions

Number of years	Rate of return		
	5%	6%	8%
10	12.58	13.18	14.49
15	21.58	23.28	27.15
20	33.07	36.79	45.76
25	47.73	54.86	73.11
30	66.44	79.06	113.28
35	90.32	111.43	172.32
40	120.80	154.76	259.06

For example, if you plan to contribute $1200 a year to your RRSP for the next 20 years, with a projected 5-percent annual return, you would multiply $1200 by 33.07 to determine the value of the funds in your plan at the end of that time. The result is $39,684.

20
Traps to Avoid

As with any type of investment, there are always things that can go wrong with your RRSP. But many of the potential pitfalls are avoidable. Here are some to watch out for:

Early conversion. You do not have to convert your RRSP to a RRIF or annuity before December 31 of the year in which you turn 71. It doesn't matter whether you retire long before then; all that counts is your age.

However, there may be a tax advantage to converting a small part of your RRSP to a RRIF at age 65. You're allowed to claim up to $2000 as a pension tax credit, which is worth $300 off your federal tax payable. If you do not have an employer pension plan, you can use income from a RRIF to qualify for this benefit (lump-sum RRSP withdrawals are not eligible).

You're allowed to convert part of an RRSP to a RRIF and keep the rest intact, so if you can benefit from this tax break, do so. But only convert the amount you need to be able to take out $2000 annually—and no more. The reason is simple.

Once you move the money into a RRIF, you are required to make minimum withdrawals each year and pay tax on the money at full rate. If you don't need the cash, you'll be paying tax prematurely and depleting the tax-sheltered savings in the account.

Keeping the money in an RRSP gives you the freedom to do what you want. If you need some cash, you can take it from the plan. If not, it can continue to grow until you reach age 71.

Tax-free withdrawals. If you see an ad promising tax-free RRSP withdrawals, ignore it—or better yet, report it to the CRA. There is no legal way to take money out of an RRSP tax-free, but scam artists keep hooking unsuspecting victims by claiming they have found a sure-fire technique to do it.

A typical deal works like this. The promoter convinces you to use the money in a self-directed plan to buy shares in a private corporation. The funds used to purchase the shares are then lent back to you at little or no interest, outside the plan. You end up with an RRSP with only the private company shares as assets. The cash is in your bank account. The promoter charges you a fee for this service and moves on. You figure that even if the shares turn out to be worthless, it doesn't matter because you have the money safely tucked away.

Here's the catch: The shares are probably not qualified RRSP investments. If the CRA finds out—and the odds are that it will since the plan administrator must report to the government each year—the value of the shares will be added to your taxable income. If it is determined that you were a willing participant in a fraud, you'll probably face a hefty fine as well.

A variation on this scheme is to use the assets of the RRSP as security on a loan made to you outside the plan. However, it's illegal to use RRSPs as loan collateral. If you do, the value of the entire RRSP will be added to your income and you'll be taxed accordingly.

Supersized contributions. It's not so common these days thanks to a CRA crackdown, but some con artists may still try to persuade you to participate in a plan that supposedly will result in an RRSP contribution that's worth several times the amount you actually put in. The pitch may be that if you buy shares in a private company, invest in a mortgage, or acquire units in a co-op in your self-directed plan, you'll get a receipt for several times the actual amount spent.

"In some cases, the promoter walks away with all the funds and cannot be found," the CRA said in a 2009 Tax Alert. "Many Canadians have lost their entire retirement savings to unscrupulous promoters by participating in such arrangements."

To that point, the CRA said that it has reassessed more than 5000 people who took part in illegal RRSP schemes, adding more than $250 million to their taxable incomes.

RRSP meltdowns. This approach to getting money out of an RRSP "tax-free" is not illegal—it's simply sleight of hand. In this case, you are encouraged to borrow money, perhaps on a home equity line of credit, and invest the proceeds in mutual funds. Because the loan is used for investment purposes, the income is tax-deductible.

You then withdraw an amount from your RRSP equal to the interest payable on the loan. The withdrawal is taxable, but the amount owed is offset by the interest deductibility. The result is a "tax-free" RRSP withdrawal.

Of course, it's smoke and mirrors. You do have to pay tax on the withdrawal. If you took no money out of the plan, you'd be able to use the interest deductibility against other income.

You've also put yourself in a potentially dangerous financial position. Borrowing to invest is called leveraging, and it's a two-edged sword. When markets are strong, it can significantly increase your profits. But if things go wrong, you could lose thousands of dollars. Imagine if you'd entered into this kind of arrangement just before the 2008 market crash. You'd probably still be in the red.

High-yield securities. We all want good returns from our investments. But if a security looks too good to be true, as the saying goes, it probably is.

Investors have been particularly frustrated by the prolonged period of low interest rates. Traditional RRSP holdings such as GICs and money market funds have offered minimal returns, leaving people scrambling for yield.

In this situation, it's tempting to look for high-yield securities if you have a self-directed plan. Something that offers a distribution of 8 percent annually looks mighty attractive when the best you can get from a GIC is 2.5 percent.

Be very wary. Remember that one of the classic rules of investing is that the greater the potential return, the higher the risk. No one gives money away. If a security is offering a high yield, there's a good reason—most likely that the chances of loss are significant. The markets factor risk into the price of every security and rarely make mistakes.

As I said earlier in the book, an RRSP is your personal pension plan and should be managed accordingly. That means not taking undue risks—if you lose money in an RRSP, it's gone forever. So think carefully before you succumb to the siren song of a high-yield security.

Deferred sales charges. A couple of years ago a reader of my *Zoomer* magazine columns wrote to ask if I had ever written about what he called "the undisclosed traps of RRSP and RRIF investing in mutual funds on a DSC basis."

He went on to describe a very costly series of events that he and his wife had experienced. Acting on the recommendations of a financial adviser, they had invested $220,000 in mutual funds, using a DSC purchase option. This means that no sales commission is payable up front; however, if you sell your units within a certain time frame (up to seven years after purchase is typical), you will be hit with a sales commission. The percentage of the commission declines the longer you remain invested.

For example, Mackenzie Financial Corporation, one of the country's largest mutual fund companies, charges a DSC fee of 5.5 percent of the current value if the units are redeemed within the first year. In the second and third years, the rate is 5 percent. In years four and five, it drops to 4 percent, goes to

3 percent in year six, and finishes at 2 percent in year seven. After that, you're off the hook.

It's important to note that the DSC is calculated on the current market value, not on the original purchase price. In times when stock markets are rising, this will have the effect of inflating your sales charge. For example, suppose you invest $10,000 in a Mackenzie equity fund and hold it for four years. The markets are good during that period, and the fund gains an average of 8 percent annually, bringing its total value to $13,605. You decide you want to take your profit and sell.

At that point, you will be hit with a DSC of $544.20 (4 percent of the current value). That's 36 percent more than if the calculation had been based on the original amount invested. The effect is that the fund company claws back some of the profit you made while you held the units.

Of course, if the fund loses money, the current value formula works in your favour. But no one invests in anything with the expectation of losing money.

It does happen, though, and that's when a DSC strikes many people as adding insult to injury. Look at the crash of 2008–2009. During the first half of 2008, markets were very strong—in fact, the Toronto Stock Exchange hit an all-time high in June. Many investors were piling into mutual funds at that point with the expectation of more gains to come.

Instead, stocks went into a death spiral. By early March 2009, the S&P/TSX Composite Index had lost about half its value. Frightened investors were bailing out of their equity funds, and being hit with high fees for doing so if they'd had the misfortune of buying them on a DSC basis. It's one thing to get dinged when you make a profit; it's quite another to have to fork over hundreds of dollars more after having been whacked by the markets.

What made the reader even angrier about his situation is that about 18 months after he and his wife made their initial investment, their adviser sold his "book" (effectively, his practice) to someone else. This is the usual practice in the industry when someone retires.

Their new adviser immediately recommended selling $63,000 worth of the equity funds in the RRIFs and switching to fixed-income securities. "We would have to absorb a 5.5 percent early redemption penalty, which we knew nothing about at the time and the second adviser did not bring it to our attention," the reader wrote.

After reading this, you may wonder why anyone would buy funds on a DSC basis. Actually, as with so many other things, it seemed like a good idea at the time. Back in the late 1980s, mutual fund sales were stagnating, largely because of the high cost of entry. At that time, funds were sold on a front-end load basis, which meant you paid an upfront commission that could be as high as 9 percent. (There were a few no-load funds, but they were not heavily promoted.) Then Mackenzie Financial came up with a new idea, created by founder Jim O'Donnell: offer a type of fund that carried no upfront commission at all. People loved it and the industry boomed. Growth in the 1990s outstripped anything ever seen before in Canada, all thanks to the DSC.

Financial advisers were onside right from the beginning. Not only were sales boosted but also their compensation. They received an upfront commission for selling DSC units that was more than they got from the traditional front-end load funds. Today, an adviser receives a 5 percent commission when you buy most Mackenzie funds on a DSC basis, whereas the payment for a front-end load purchase is likely to be lower since that has to be negotiated with the client. Advisers also receive an annual "trailer fee" for services rendered of between 0.15 percent and 1.25 percent, depending on the type of fund unit purchased. Money market funds earn the lowest fees, followed by fixed-income funds (usually 0.5 percent), equity and balanced funds (1 percent), and portfolio funds (as high as 1.25 percent).

This means financial advisers have a vested interest in encouraging you to buy equity, balanced, or portfolio funds on a DSC basis and holding on to them forever. Never forget this when you are listening to your adviser's recommendations.

What can you do to avoid or reduce these costs? Here are some ideas:

• *The low-load option.* There is a less-expensive form of DSC, known as low-load. Your adviser may not tell you about it because the sales commissions are lower—typically half of what is paid on a regular DSC purchase. But if you must buy on a DSC basis, low-load is the way to go. In the case of Mackenzie Financial (which is typical in the industry), the redemption charge is only 3 percent in year one,

2.5 percent in year two, and 2 percent in year three. After that, you can sell at no cost.

- *Zero commission front-end load.* Most discount brokers and many full-service advisers now offer front-end load units at zero commission. They forego the sales commission in doing so, but are compensated by the annual trailer fees. This is a good deal for you: You won't have to lay out any cash up front and will avoid potential DSC charges down the road.

- *Fee-based accounts.* Many brokers now encourage clients to move to a fee-based account. This involves paying an annual fee of perhaps 1.5 percent on the value of your portfolio. In return, you receive commission-free stock trading and are entitled to use F-class mutual fund units. These are sold with no commission and pay no trailer fees, so the ongoing carrying cost (known as the fund's management expense ratio or MER) is much lower.

- *No-load funds.* Finally, you can avoid sales commissions altogether (but not necessarily trailer fees) by using no-load funds. In contrast to the situation in the 1980s, there are plenty from which to choose. All the banks offer them, and in fact, Royal Bank is now the biggest mutual fund seller in the country, through its RBC funds.

In the end, it comes down to savvy shopping. There is no reason to lock into DSC funds today; there are lots of other options available. It's just a matter of understanding how the business works.

21
The Transition Phase

It may seem like a long way off right now, but the time will come when you have to wind up your RRSP. That has to be done by December 31 of the year in which you turn 71. At that point, you will have four options:

Withdraw all the money in cash. You can take the money and run, but unless the RRSP is very small, I don't advise it. The cash-out will be treated as income and taxed accordingly. Depending on your tax bracket, you could end up giving a big chunk of it to the government.

Use the capital in your plan to purchase an annuity. This will provide regular income until age 90 (a term annuity) or for life (a life annuity), depending on which type you select. You'll find more information on annuities in chapter 23.

Transfer your RRSP assets into a RRIF. This is the preferred choice of most Canadians, at least in the early years of retirement.

Convert to a Life Income Fund (LIF) or Locked-in Retirement Income Fund (LRIF). These options are available to someone with a locked-in RRSP, also known as a locked-in retirement account (LIRA).

The choices are not mutually exclusive. You might decide to combine an annuity with a RRIF or LIF, or even cash in some of your RRSP assets at age 71 if your personal situation makes it desirable. Indeed, combining your conversion options could be the best strategy in certain situations.

Although the windup doesn't have to take place until you're 71, it's important to start the transition much earlier. With careful planning, your RRSP can be well positioned to make the switch in a seamless manner when the time comes.

The first step is to gradually reduce the degree of risk in the plan as you get older. As I explained in chapter 6, this process should begin at about age 50 and continue in stages until you retire or reach age 71. During this time, you should keep two goals in mind:

1. *Protect your capital.* The last thing you want is to suffer a serious financial blow a couple of years before you plan to retire, which is exactly what happened to some people when the stock market crashed in 2008–2009.
2. *Properly position your RRSP.* At age 71, your plan should be structured so as to allow for an easy transition to the next stage. If you intend to convert to a RRIF or LIF, you'll want a portfolio that places the emphasis on cash flow and asset protection. If

you plan to withdraw the money or purchase an annuity, most or all of the assets should be in cash.

The reason for the long transition period is to avoid being whipsawed by market shocks. Forward planning enables you to buy and sell assets at propitious times rather than becoming a prisoner to market forces.

A few years before you reach age 71, you should start consolidating all your RRSPs into a single plan. Many people have two or more RRSPs scattered around. Whether your final goal is a RRIF or an annuity, having a single RRSP will make the changeover easier.

Of course, you could convert each RRSP to a separate RRIF if you wish, but it's not a good idea. Multiple RRIFs are harder to manage, and you have to take a minimum payment from each plan. You may also end up paying more in administrative charges than necessary.

Asset Mix

It's essential to realize that the traditional asset mix formulas for RRSPs don't work when cash flow becomes a primary concern, as it will after you retire. A completely different asset mix is required for that purpose.

Complicating the issue is the question of risk. It would be relatively easy to put together a portfolio that generates cash flow of 8 percent to 10 percent, even in times of low interest rates. There are a lot of high-yielding stocks out there that will do the job. But this would entail a large measure of risk, which many income investors would be unwilling to accept. So the challenge is to find the right balance and to start putting it in place early.

Here are several types of income securities, listed in ascending order of risk:

Cash-type securities. These include treasury bills, money market funds, bankers' acceptances, term deposits, high-yield savings accounts, Canada Savings and Canada Premium bonds, and similar securities. The return potential depends on what interest rates are doing. When rates are low, the returns from this category will be minimal. Offsetting that is the fact that these securities rank at the top of the safety scale.

Mortgage-backed securities (MBSs). These are just about as safe as treasury bills because they are guaranteed for principal and interest by Canada Mortgage and Housing, a Crown corporation. As long as you hold them to maturity, you won't lose your capital, and, unlike GICs, there is no limit on the guarantee. MBSs are useful for those seeking steady income with very little risk, so they are well suited to retirees. However, returns will be minimal when interest rates are low.

Guaranteed investment certificates. Traditional GICs are very safe, especially those covered by deposit insurance. Any certificate from a member of the Canada Deposit Insurance Corporation (CDIC) with a value up to $100,000 qualifies. GICs issued by credit unions are covered by provincial insurance plans. For cash flow purposes, monthly-pay GICs are the best choice, although they usually offer a lower return.

Short-term bonds and funds. Short-term bonds have a maturity date of no more than five years from the time of purchase. These bonds are highly defensive, which means their market value is not severely affected by interest-rate movements, up or down. As a result, they offer good protection in a rising-interest-rate climate, as do the mutual funds and ETFs that invest in them. As a general rule, the shorter the term to maturity, the lower the risk. Canada bonds are the safest, but AA- or AAA-rated corporate issues are almost as good and will give you a better return.

Mid-term bonds. Here we are looking at maturities of 5 to 10 years. The yields are higher, but so is the risk.

Long-term bonds. This is a classic case of higher returns, higher risk. Bonds with a maturity date of more than 10 years in the future normally offer the best yields, but if interest rates move higher, their market value is likely to decline, perhaps significantly.

High-yield bonds. These so-called junk bonds don't follow the general pattern of government and highly rated corporate bonds. Interest rate movements aren't the primary force here. What counts is the creditworthiness of the issuing companies. In times of economic stress, the risk of default mounts as credit ratings are downgraded, and these bonds may drop in value accordingly.

Preferred shares. They normally (but not always) provide a better yield than the dividends paid by common shares. The payments are eligible for the dividend tax credit if the shares are held outside a registered plan.

Income mutual funds/ETFs. In response to growing demand from older Canadians, there has been an explosion in the number of income-paying mutual funds and ETFs in recent years. Many of these offer monthly payouts, but before you buy, make sure the distribution is sustainable. If the fund has a history of declining net asset value (NAV), a distribution cut could be in the offing.

Income trusts/REITs/limited partnerships. There are still a few income trusts around despite the government crackdown that took effect in 2011. You can expect better cash flow from these securities than from a bond, but the risk is much higher.

Dividend-paying common stocks. Generally, investors buy stocks for their capital gains potential, not for cash flow, although some stocks pay decent dividends, notably banks, telecoms, and utilities.

As a general rule, the more risk you are prepared to assume, the higher your potential cash flow. However, it's important to find the right balance. If you want a significant amount of capital protection, go heavy on treasury bills, mortgage-backed securities, GICs, and short-term bonds. Conversely, you could increase returns by reducing the weighting in those categories and adding more high-yield bonds, REITs, etc., but your risk factor would rise accordingly.

Obviously, there are a lot of moving parts here. That's why it's important to begin the process early and not wait until the last minute.

22
Converting to a RRIF

A RRIF differs from an RRSP in two fundamental ways: First, you cannot make new contributions to a RRIF; additional money can only come from other registered plans. Second, you must make taxable minimum annual withdrawals from a RRIF, according to a formula laid down by the federal government. These withdrawals must begin no later than the calendar year following the date the plan is set up. So, if you open your RRIF at any time in 2014, you must start making withdrawals no later than 2015.

Other than that, a RRIF functions in much the same way as an RRSP. You can hold the same kinds of assets, you may have a self-directed plan, and you'll pay similar fees. Some of the benefits of a RRIF include the following:

Control of capital. You keep the capital you've built over the years. If you purchase an annuity, the money is paid over to a life insurance company.

Withdrawal flexibility. While you must take out a minimum amount each year, you have the flexibility to withdraw as much as you wish from the plan. This allows for large lump-sum withdrawals in the early years of retirement, when you may wish to travel more. You may also change your withdrawal formula at any time to meet current needs.

Inflation protection. You may set up your income stream from a RRIF in such a way that the amount you draw increases each year. This will enable you to keep pace with higher living costs.

Estate planning. Assets remaining in a RRIF after death will form part of the estate (unless they pass to a named beneficiary of the plan). They will therefore be available to your spouse, children, other relatives, or your favourite charity once appropriate taxes have been paid. Unless you have purchased a guarantee clause, annuity payments cease when you die or, in the case of a joint annuity, when the surviving spouse dies.

If you decide to go the RRIF route, here are three important points to consider:

1. *How much income do I need from my RRIF?* Review your planned expenses and other sources of income. See how much you need from your RRIF in order to maintain your desired standard of living. Your goal should be to withdraw as little as possible from your retirement fund.
2. *How often do I need this income?* If you require a monthly cheque in order to pay the bills, that can be arranged. But if you can wait until year-end and

receive just one annual payment, you'll continue to maximize the tax-sheltered growth in your plan. If you have more than one RRIF, or you and your spouse each has one, you may wish to set up a different payment schedule for each to ensure regular income.

3. *Will my investments provide the cash flow I need?* A five-year compounding GIC won't generate any income for you because it's locked in. Neither will shares in a growth company that pays no dividends. At this point in your life, income needs must take precedence over growth in your investment decisions. Adjust the plan accordingly.

Minimum RRIF/LIF Withdrawals

The government requires you to withdraw a minimum amount from a RRIF or LIF annually, and this amount is fully taxable at your marginal rate. There is no way around this rule. I receive several questions every year from people asking how to minimize the taxes on RRIF withdrawals, and the answer is always the same: You can't. There are various schemes for offsetting the tax payable by deductions of different types, but these tend to be quite complex and, in many cases, legally questionable. Be careful.

The method for calculating the minimum withdrawal requirement depends on your age. If you are under age 71, apply the following formula:

$$\text{Minimum withdrawal} = \frac{\text{Value of RRIF at start of year}}{90 - \text{Your age at start of year}}$$

So, if you had $100,000 in a RRIF at the beginning of 2014 and you were age 70, the minimum withdrawal would be calculated as follows:

$$\frac{\$100,000}{90 - 70} = \frac{\$100,000}{20} = \$5000$$

Once you reach age 71, the formula no longer applies. Instead, the minimum is a percentage of the capital in the plan at the beginning of each year, as shown in the following table.

Minimum Annual RRIF Withdrawals

Age	Minimum withdrawal (%)
71	7.38
72	7.48
73	7.59
74	7.71
75	7.85
76	7.99
77	8.15
78	8.33
79	8.53
80	8.75
81	8.99
82	9.27

Age	Minimum withdrawal (%)
83	9.58
84	9.93
85	10.33
86	10.79
87	11.33
88	11.96
89	12.71
90	13.62
91	14.73
92	16.12
93	17.92
94+	20.00

At age 94, the minimum annual payment reaches 20 percent of the value of the RRIF at the start of each year, and remains at that level for the rest of your life. Although this ensures there will be money available after age 90, the formula poses another problem. The large percentage of the RRIF's assets that must be paid out each year will quickly erode the capital base of the plan. As a result, the amount you'll receive each year will steadily decline as you reach your mid-90s, as the table below shows. For this illustration, I've assumed the RRIF is worth $100,000 at age 90, and that income is earned on the capital at the rate of 6 percent a year. For simplicity, it is assumed that the minimum annual withdrawal is made in one lump sum at year-end (it won't often happen that way in real life, but this is just an example).

Annual Withdrawals after Age 90

Age	RRIF value, Jan. 1	Minimum withdrawl (%)	Payment	Income earned that year
90	$100,000	13.62	$13,620	$6000
91	$ 92,380	14.73	$13,608	$5543
92	$ 84,315	16.12	$13,592	$5059
93	$ 75,782	17.92	$13,580	$4547
94	$ 66,749	20.00	$13,350	$4005
95	$ 57,404	20.00	$11,481	$3444
96	$ 49,367	20.00	$ 9873	$2962
97	$ 42,456	20.00	$ 8491	$2547
98	$ 36,512	20.00	$ 7302	$2191
99	$ 31,401	20.00	$ 6280	$1884
100	$ 27,005	20.00	$ 5401	$1620

For a retiree relying solely on RRIF income to live, this type of scenario could be financially devastating. As you can see, by the time you reach the age of 100, your income is about 60 percent less than what it was just six years earlier. Your reaction may be: "So what! If I live that long, I won't care anyway." Maybe not, but your family will certainly be affected if faced with an increased financial burden because you didn't plan for this contingency.

So as you get older, don't put all your retirement eggs in the RRIF basket. You'll need some other sources of income if you live to a ripe old age. One alternative would be to convert part or all the capital in the RRIF to a life annuity when you're in your late 80s. This will ensure regular income for as long as you live. More on this in the next chapter.

Setting Up a RRIF

Setting up a RRIF is relatively simple, at least on the surface. Just visit the financial institution, broker, or planner who handles your RRSP, say you want to convert to a RRIF, and sign the documents that will be provided. Presto, it's done.

But creating a RRIF that will do exactly the job you want it to do is something else again. That process requires some careful planning and preparation, and there are several steps involved. Here's my Seven-Step RRIF-Creation Strategy:

Step 1: Decide how much cash flow you need. If you have ample income from other sources (workplace pension, CPP, investments, consulting work, etc.), aim for the minimum withdrawal to minimize the tax bite and keep as much money as possible tax-sheltered. However, if the RRIF will provide a significant portion of your retirement income, you may have to take out more than the minimum to allow you to maintain your standard of living. Any RRIF adviser should be able to provide a computer printout showing the effect of various levels of withdrawal on your plan. Assuming a constant rate of investment return within the RRIF, the more money you take out, the faster the capital in the plan will be depleted. Be sure to study the figures carefully, checking to see when the income from the plan starts to decline at the withdrawal level you're considering. If the plan's assets will be depleted too quickly, see if there is some alternative, perhaps by cutting living expenses, by supplementing your income with a part-time job, or by other means.

Step 2: Consolidate your RRSPs into a single plan. Many people have more than one RRSP. There's nothing wrong with that, but as mentioned in the previous chapter, it's not a good idea to carry that over to your RRIF. It's difficult to manage several RRIFs, and you must take a minimum payment from each plan. In this situation, choose your RRIF provider with great care. Every company with which you have an RRSP will want your business, but be selective. Have discussions with a representative of each organization before you decide. Ask about the RRIF services they offer, and the fees you'll be charged. Insist on seeing a sample account statement, and study it carefully to make sure it contains all the necessary information. This should include the current balance of the account, a record of withdrawals, and an itemized statement of assets, including the book value and current market price. Find out how often the statement is issued (monthly is best). If you plan to travel a lot, see what snowbird services the company provides.

Step 3: Decide if you want the RRIF assets to be professionally managed. Most financial institutions and brokerage firms now offer this service. Charges are usually based on a percentage of the RRIF assets. This will cost more than doing it yourself, but it should save a lot of time and headaches.

Step 4: Decide what type of RRIF you want. Like RRSPs, there are several different types of plans. You'll get maximum flexibility from a self-directed RRIF. For minimum maintenance, lowest cost, and maximum safety, a RRIF based on GICs or Canada Premium Bonds will be most effective, although not the most profitable by any means.

Step 5: Make the "fine print" decisions. When you set up your RRIF, you have the choice of basing the minimum annual withdrawals on your own age or the age of your spouse if he or she is younger. If the younger-spouse situation applies, you should always select it because it provides more flexibility and lower tax liability. There is no limit on how young the spouse can be. If you're a 70-year-old retired teacher who has just married a 30-year-old former student, use his or her age by all means. On a $100,000 RRIF, you'd have to withdraw (and pay tax on) $5000 in the first year if you use your age. By using the 30-year-old spouse's age, the minimum withdrawal would be only $1667. Of course, this is an extreme example, but it dramatically illustrates the point. If you don't need the money right away, better that it stays in the plan and continues to earn tax-sheltered income. Using the age of a younger spouse is the best way to achieve this, even if the differential is only a few years.

Designate your spouse or partner as the beneficiary to your plan. This means your spouse will inherit the assets in the plan tax-free and that the RRIF will not be subject to probate.

Arrange for direct transfer of the payments to your bank

account. That way you are assured timely receipt of the money.

Decide on the amount of tax you want withheld from your payments. (If you don't give instructions, the withholding rates that apply to RRSP withdrawals will prevail.) But to avoid a big tax bill the following April, it's a good idea to estimate what your marginal tax rate will be, and ask the plan administrator to withhold that percentage.

Step 6: Decide on your investment portfolio. The big difference between a RRIF and an RRSP is that your emphasis switches from growth to income. So the assets in the plan will have to be structured to provide the cash flow needed for the RRIF to dispense regular payments to you. The frequency of the cheques or direct transfers is up to you; it need be only once a year if you wish. You should also place more importance on capital preservation than you may have in the past. You cannot contribute any more money to a RRIF, so it's essential to ensure that your capital isn't eroded by unwise investments.

Step 7: Consider tax-reduction strategies. Payments from a RRIF will be taxed at your marginal rate. No tax breaks are available, regardless of the original source of the money. So, for example, dividends earned inside the RRIF will not qualify for the dividend tax credit when withdrawn. Therefore, be sure to maximize the tax efficiency between your registered and non-registered portfolios. If you are holding dividend-paying stocks or income trusts inside your

RRIF and have interest-bearing securities outside the plan, you are paying more tax than you should be.

If you don't need all the money you receive from a RRIF each year, put the balance into a TFSA. That way, future investment earnings will be protected.

23
The Annuity Option

Like many people, I wouldn't mind living to 100 as long as I could have two wishes. My first wish is that my health, both physical and mental, stays reasonably good. My second is that my money lasts as long as I do so that I can continue to enjoy the lifestyle to which I'm accustomed. As we saw in the last chapter, a RRIF won't do that for you.

You'll have to look elsewhere for advice on staying healthy to 100 and beyond. My job is to explain how to make sure you don't run out of money. No one wants to spend their final years depending on their children or the charity of others to survive.

Unless you're a multi-millionaire or win the lottery, there is only one sure way to ensure that you will have enough income to live comfortably for as long as you're around. That is to use some of your RRSP savings to purchase a life annuity.

Annuities can come with all sorts of bells and whistles. But when you strip those away, a life annuity is simply a contract between you and a life insurance company under which it agrees to pay you regular income for as long as you live, however long that may be. The insurance companies employ teams of high-powered actuaries who figure out to the month how long people in various age groups are likely to survive, and they base their rates on those projections. If you die early or on schedule, the insurance company wins. If you live well beyond your normal life expectancy, you win. In a sense, it's something of a gamble. The constant that makes it worth taking is the fact that you'll continue to receive regular payments, no matter how long you live. You should never have to worry about where the next cheque is coming from.

Annuities have fallen out of favour in recent years because of two factors: low interest rates, which reduce the income you'll receive for your capital, and the desire of older Canadians to retain control over their assets and leave something for their children when they go.

Despite this, I have consistently advised readers of my retirement books to consider buying an annuity when they reach their 80s. The reason is simple: As we saw in the previous chapter, under current minimum withdrawal rules, the capital in RRIFs and LIFs will rapidly be depleted after that. At age 80, the federal government requires you to withdraw 8.75 percent of a RRIF's annual opening value. By 85, the minimum is up to 10.33 percent, by 90 it has reached 13.62 percent, and after 94 it is 20 percent a year.

In the previous chapter there was an analysis of what would happen to a $100,000 RRIF after age 90, assuming a 6 percent average annual return on capital. As we saw, starting at age 95, the capital in the RRIF steadily depleted, as did the amount of income received each year. By age 100, the RRIF annuitant would receive only about 40 percent of the amount that was paid at age 94.

The solution is to buy a life annuity while you are in your

80s. I suggest waiting that long because the older you are when you enter into a contract, the higher your payments will be. Apart from your age, the amount of the payment will vary depending on five factors: the amount of money you invest, your sex (men get more than women because they tend to die sooner), the level of interest rates when you make the purchase (the higher, the better), the type of annuity you choose, and the life insurance company you deal with.

When you go shopping for an annuity, you'll need to keep your wits about you. Like most insurance products, they tend to be much more complicated than necessary and apples-to-apples comparisons between companies can be difficult. There are three basic types of life annuities: single male, single female, and joint. The latter continues to make payments until the death of the last surviving spouse.

But that's just the beginning. You will be offered guaranteed annuities (payments will be made for the guarantee period even if you die), indexed annuities (payments increase with inflation), impaired annuities (you have a health condition that makes it probable you will die soon), and more. Except in the case of impaired annuities, the more options you choose, the less cash you will receive each month.

The GlobeInvestor website has a feature that enables you to check current prices for various types of basic annuities. Go to www.globeinvestor.com, click on "Personal Finance" and then "Rates." You'll find quotes from several insurance companies based on age and the type of annuity you choose. The figures are monthly payments per $100,000 invested.

However, don't assume the numbers are up-to-the-minute. Check with a representative of the companies you're interested in to obtain an official quote.

I visited the site at the time of writing to check on quotes for buying an annuity using money from a registered plan. I found that the best payout for a single male with no guarantee was from Empire Life. At age 70, the monthly cheque would be $683.81, but by waiting until age 75 to buy the annuity, it would increase to $817.86.

If he opted for a 10-year guarantee, meaning payments would continue to his heirs if he died during the period, the best quote was from Sun Life, which offered monthly cheques of $631.89 for a 70-year-old and $710.97 for a 75-year-old. The longer the guarantee period, the less the monthly payment.

For a single female with no guarantee, Standard Life came in best. They were offering $611.96 a month at age 70. But at age 75, Empire Life was best at $708.65 a month, which shows the importance of careful research before deciding.

For a joint annuity with no guarantee, Sun Life was best with monthly payments of $527.79 at age 70 and $598.78 at age 75.

Be sure to do your homework before making a decision on which company to deal with. Payout rates can vary significantly from one life insurer to another, and the best-paying company for one type of annuity may not be the same as for a different type. It's a maze. If you need help finding your way through it, contact an annuity broker. You can locate one in your area through a Google search.

Remember that there are downsides to annuities. For starters, you surrender your capital to buy one. Once you hand over your $100,000 or whatever amount, it's gone. You no longer have it to invest or to pass on as part of an inheritance, which is why many people choose guarantees even though they reduce the monthly payment. Also, when interest rates are low, annuities become more expensive in terms of what you get for your money. If you can wait, do so.

Also, don't lose sight of the fact that if the insurance company you deal with runs into financial problems, your annuity could be affected. There is an industry-run organization called Assuris, which provides protection up to a maximum of $2000 a month if the annuity provider fails, but any amounts beyond that are at risk. You'll find more details at www.assuris.ca.

Annuity Terms

Before you start shopping, here are some terms you need to understand when looking for a life annuity. Not all companies offer all these options, and the names may differ for marketing reasons.

Single annuity. This is issued to you personally. Payments will be calculated on the basis of your life expectancy.

Joint life annuity (also called last survivor annuity). This type of plan guarantees payment for both you and your spouse (or partner) that will continue for as long as one of you remains alive.

Guarantee. A promise from the issuing company that you or your estate will receive a specified amount of money, no matter what happens. Think of it as a form of insurance. If you die without a guarantee the month after you purchase an annuity, your heirs will receive nothing. With a guarantee, they'll at least get a return equal to the amount you would have been paid over the guarantee period. This may be paid either in instalments or as a lump sum, depending on the terms you choose. A typical guarantee will run for 5, 10, or 15 years, although some companies offer them for longer periods. The longer the guarantee you choose, the less your income payments will be. In effect, you'll pay a higher premium for a longer guarantee.

Many financial advisers recommend you take a guarantee, especially if you're buying a single annuity. But it's very costly, and the amount of protection you're receiving declines every year. It's also one of the few forms of insurance I'm aware of where the premiums continue long after the coverage runs out (you'll continue to receive the lower payment even after the guarantee expires).

Only you can decide if it's worth it, but the younger you are and the better your health, the less chance your heirs will ever benefit from the guarantee. If you're buying a joint annuity and you're both in good health, I suggest you seriously consider bypassing the guarantee; odds are that at least one of you will outlive it.

Impaired annuities. If you're in poor health when you apply for a life insurance policy, chances are you won't get coverage. If you do, you're likely to be charged a premium rate. With an annuity, however, poor health can translate into a financial advantage. If your medical report indicates that your life expectancy is below normal, some companies will issue what's known as an impaired annuity. You'll receive higher monthly payments (perhaps by as much as 15 percent) for your money. The trick is to then turn around and surprise them by living far longer than anyone expected!

Increasing income and indexed annuities. There are two basic types of income-protection annuities available. One is known as an increasing life annuity. This type of plan increases your payment by a set percentage each year, usually between 1 percent and 4 percent, regardless of movements in the consumer price index. Alternatively, you can choose an indexed annuity. This plan will increase your payments each year in line with the inflation rate, although some companies put a cap on the amount of annual increase that's allowed.

With both these annuities, your initial income will be much lower than you'd receive with an ordinary, level-payment plan. However, you'll make up for that initial shortfall over time as your payments increase—assuming, of course, that you live long enough.

If you don't have any other inflation protection in your retirement income program, you should look carefully at these annuity options. No one should begin retirement with an income that will remain relatively constant, unless it's much more than you initially need and you can afford to keep adding to your savings.

Income-reducing annuities. Payments from these joint annuities decline when the first spouse dies, on the somewhat dubious theory that one can live more cheaply than two. The income for the surviving spouse may drop by anywhere from one-third to three-quarters of the original payment. There's potential for genuine financial hardship for your loved one in arrangements like this. Suppose, for example, he or she needs expensive medical care in old age or has to live in an assisted-care facility. Cutting the annuity payment substantially may make that difficult or impossible. These plans aren't particularly popular, with good reason.

Integrated annuities. These are structured in such a way that the payments are reduced on a dollar-for-dollar basis as the CPP and OAS benefits kick in. The result is a level income for life. Integrated annuities are most useful to people who retire early and need higher monthly payments to tide them over until they are eligible to begin drawing government benefits.

Variable annuities. These plans invest your money in a fund, with your payments based on the fund's performance. Because of this unpredictability factor, they shouldn't be considered if you're relying on this money as the prime source of your income.

Cashable annuities. At one time, an annuity, like a diamond, was forever. Once you were in, there was no going back. The decision was made and you had to live with it. Now, however, you can keep your financial options open with a cashable annuity. If you decide you want to get out, you can arrange to have your annuity cashed in (the technical term is "commuted") at its current value. At that point, you can use the money to buy another annuity or to invest in a RRIF, in which case no tax will be payable. Or you can have the cash paid directly to you, as long as you don't mind paying tax on it at your top rate. As with everything else in the annuity world, you have to pay for this flexibility in the form of lower monthly payments.

Renewable annuities. Normally, the interest rate on which your annuity payments are based is locked in for the duration of the plan. However, it is now possible to buy an annuity for which the period of the rate guarantee is shorter than the term of the plan. At the end of each interest-rate period, you can use your remaining cash value to buy another renewable annuity, a life or fixed-term annuity, or a RRIF. This type of annuity is worth considering if interest rates are low at the time of your purchase. Rather than lock in a low rate for the rest of your life, a renewable annuity enables you to choose a shorter term in the hope rates will be higher when the time comes to renew. Usually, however, the shorter the term you select, the lower the interest rate paid and, therefore, the less income you'll receive. Again, you pay for flexibility.

Deferred annuities. One way to avoid the problems created by annuity shopping when interest rates are down is to buy a deferred annuity when rates are high. This is the life insurance industry's equivalent of a GIC. The primary difference from an ordinary GIC that you'd buy from a bank or trust company is that with a deferred annuity, the proceeds from the plan must be used to purchase an annuity (or be redeemed) by a specific date. This may be a specific number of years, or it may relate to the investor's age.

Remember, the level of interest rates is an extremely important factor in buying an annuity. If you lock in for a long term at a time when rates are low, you'll end up sacrificing thousands of dollars in retirement income. So time your annuity purchases for maximum return. If interest rates are low when you're shopping, postpone the decision or buy a renewable annuity, which will allow you to get back into the market under more propitious circumstances.

So yes, there is a way to be sure you won't outlive your money even if you're around to blow out 100 birthday candles. Just make sure you stay healthy enough to enjoy it.

24

Your RRSP Questions

Every year, I receive dozens of questions about RRSPs and RRIFs. Some deal with very simple matters, and the answers could easily be found by going to the Canada Revenue Agency website or doing a Google search. Others, however, can be very complex, sometimes raising issues that had not even occurred to me. Here is a selection of some of the more interesting queries I've received, grouped by general topic.

General RRSP Questions

DAUGHTER WANTS TO OPEN RRSP

Q My daughter is turning 18. This summer, she started her very first summer job. I'd like to assist her in opening up her own RRSP account. I wonder if, in her case, she can use the $2000 lifetime RRSP overcontribution strategy to start her savings this year.

A The overcontribution strategy won't work quite yet. She must be at least 19 to make an overcontribution to a registered plan. So she'll have to wait until her next birthday. At that point, she could make a $2000 overcontribution if she wished.

As for regular contributions, the allowable amount is based on the previous year's earned income. Since your daughter had no income last year, she has no contribution room for the current tax year. The money that she earns this summer will be used to calculate next year's RRSP contribution limit.

HOW MUCH IS TOO MUCH?

Q My wife and I are 29 and have $65,000 in RRSP savings, and approximately $10,000 in cash. At what point is too much committed to RRSPs?

A Certainly not $65,000, given your age. However, much will depend on whether or not you have a workplace pension plan. If you both have such a plan, and they are generous (increasingly rare these days), then you can afford to ease back on your RRSP savings. In this situation, the retirement income you receive from your personal savings will simply be an add-on to your pensions.

However, if you expect to rely on your RRSP for the bulk of your retirement income, you should continue to sock away as much money as possible. For example, suppose the two of you have a combined income of $75,000. You want to obtain retirement income of 80 percent of that amount at age 65, with a built-in inflation factor of 2 percent. That means your adjusted income at retirement will need to be $152,992. You want to make sure you have enough to last you for 25 years.

You decide to contribute $2500 a year to your RRSPs, earning an average annual return of 6 percent, and save another $500 a year in a non-registered portfolio, adding to the $10,000 you already have, with an average annual return of 4 percent.

With the money you already have put aside and adding in the Canada Pension Plan and Old Age Security, you will have enough to meet your goal, but just barely. You will start retirement with assets of just over $1 million, but by the time both of you are age 90, there will only be $100,000 left. If either of you lives much longer than that, there will be a problem.

So the bottom line is, keep saving!

CONSIDERING FOLDING RRSP

Q I am 33 years old and have an RRSP from previous employment worth approximately $15,000. What I am interested in doing is collapsing my RRSP and using the proceeds to pay off my non-deductible debt. What are the implications of doing such?

A First, make sure that the RRSP is not locked in. When you say it is "from previous employment," that raises some alarm bells. If the plan is locked in, you will not be able to collapse it. Some provinces allow withdrawals from locked-in plans but only under certain conditions.

If the RRSP is not locked in, very carefully check the tax implications of collapsing it. Remember that the whole amount will be added to your income in the year received. That means you will end up paying tax on the withdrawal at your marginal rate. If that rate were 40 percent, adding the extra $15,000 to your income means that $6000 of your money will go to the government.

WANTS A BIG RRSP LOAN

Q Where is the best place to obtain a large RRSP loan? Is it possible to obtain a loan for lower than prime?

A There is no "best place." My advice is to shop around. Talk to three or four possible lenders and see who offers the best terms. Some banks have special deals for people seeking large loans so they can catch up on carry-forward room that has accumulated over several years. Also, check with your financial adviser. Sometimes brokerage firms will provide special arrangements.

It is quite possible that you could obtain an RRSP loan for less than prime. Hold off until the RRSP season is in full swing, when these loans are most heavily promoted and the competition is at its highest.

TRANSFERRING RRSPs

Q I have a spousal RRSP for my wife and a separate RRSP for me (contributed to from a separation allowance when I took an early retirement). Can I transfer my RRSP into the spousal RRSP?

A No. Your RRSP is your property, but the spousal RRSP belongs to your wife. You cannot transfer your RRSP assets into another person's plan, except in a few special situations, such as marriage breakdown.

Home Buyers' Plan

WANTS TO USE RRSP TO BUY HOME

Q Is it a good idea to use my RRSP to buy a home? Do I get a tax break this current year for the money invested into our home? How does it work?

What about future years? Can I ever invest into RRSPs again and receive a tax break? If I am paying back the money withdrawn over 15 years, must the total amount be repaid before I can take advantage of tax breaks, i.e., RRSP contributions?

A You are obviously referring to the federal government's Home Buyers' Plan. This allows you to borrow up to $25,000 from an RRSP for a first-time home purchase. There is no tax break involved, but the loan is interest-free. You have to repay your RRSP over 15 years, but any contributions made to the plan over and above the loan repayment are eligible for the usual tax deduction.

LOST MONEY

Q I purchased a home four years ago and applied some of my RRSP savings towards my down payment. Knowing all the rules, I began repaying myself. My question is where has my repayment money gone? Initially I borrowed from my RRSP from one financial institution and have since closed my account and gone to another financial institution. I have never received any statement to say exactly where my money is. The only proof of payment I have is my income tax return. But now I would like to place this money and don't know where it is. Neither the government nor the bank I deal with can help me. I feel desperate and need to get some answers.

You obviously used the Home Buyers' Plan to withdraw money from your RRSP to make the down payment. Your annual repayments can be made to any RRSP you own, not necessarily the plan from which the cash originated, so the fact that you switched banks is not an issue.

You should be receiving periodic statements from the financial institution that now holds your plan. These should come at least once a year and preferably more often. If you have not received any statements, then go to your branch and insist that they provide one.

The statement should show all cash inflows into the plan, including your loan repayments. Depending on the arrangements you made when you set up the RRSP, this money may be being held as cash, or may have been automatically invested for you.

Review the statements to see if you have been credited for the loan repayments. If not, take your cancelled cheques to your bank as evidence of the payments and get them to make the appropriate adjustments.

If you continue to have problems, ask for an appointment with the manager to resolve the issue.

CONFUSED ABOUT HOME BUYERS' PLAN LOAN

We are using our RRSPs for a first-time homeowner's down payment. Our credit union tells us we have to take the full amount out of the RRSP, put it in a variable RRSP account, take what we need out of it, then put the remainder back into a new RRSP. This does not sound right to me. If you have a large RRSP at a good rate, do you have to lose the good rate to take $25,000 out of it?

A It sounds to me like you have the money in an RRSP that only allows you to hold guaranteed investment certificates. The credit union may be saying that you have to cash in one or more of those GICs and move the money into a different kind of plan in order to use the government's Home Buyers' Plan.

You certainly do not have to take the money out of your RRSP, in the sense of withdrawing it, and you should not do so, since that would make it taxable. All you are doing is transferring from one type of RRSP account to another.

It would appear that you need to get the money out of an existing GIC that is worth more than the $25,000 you want. The credit union is saying you can't take part of the amount and leave the rest in the GIC—you have to cash in the whole GIC, take the amount you need for the loan, and reinvest whatever is left. When you do that, it will be at today's rates (if you go back into a GIC, which you should think twice about). There is no other way—you can't have your cake and eat it too.

Government Services

SHOULD HE CASH RRSPs?

Q I'm approximately five years away from retirement (60 next April), with very little RRSP savings (approximately $90,000–$100,000) and an annual salary of $93,000. During my younger years I did not concentrate on "retirement" savings, and hence I'm in the position that I have identified.

In recent years I have had an investment firm advise me of my best approach but have been very unhappy with them, and currently I'm losing money. This investment firm also suggested I borrow $50,000 and invest it. This I did a couple of years back. The value of this is now around $35,000, and I still owe on the loan.

I did hear that based on my status (minimal RRSPs) and being close to retirement, I may be better off by cashing in these RRSPs since the government may penalize me for future pensions. Note: I have no private pensions.

My questions are:

a) Should I cash in my RRSPs—if yes, whom do I contact to determine the amount I will need to pay on taxes, etc.?

b) Is there a better solution?

A If you cash in your RRSPs now, you will pay tax on the proceeds at your marginal rate. Since you are in a high tax bracket, given your current salary, that means the government will take a big bite out of the proceeds. For an Ontario resident at your income level, every additional dollar will be taxed at a rate of 43.41 percent. If you collapse your RRSP right now, most of the money you withdraw will be taxed at that rate. I cannot see any sense in that.

If you didn't add any more to the RRSP, you could conservatively expect to receive between $4000 and $6000 a year from the plan once you start to draw against it, depending on how you invest the money. As far as government pensions are concerned, you have to ask yourself whether this amount will do any of these things:

1. Push your net income over the level at which the Old Age Security clawback kicks in. For 2013, that was about $71,000.
2. Affect your entitlement to collect the Guaranteed Income Supplement (GIS). I doubt you would be eligible for that anyway, since it is designed for low-income people, but if you expect the combined income of you and your spouse after retirement to fall below $22,000 a year, you need to consider this.
3. Affect your ability to claim the age tax credit, which kicks in at 65. The net income threshold in 2013 was $34,562.

Points 2 and 3 and point 1 are mutually exclusive. If you expect to have a high income after retirement, point 1 becomes a factor. If you expect your income to fall dramatically, look at points 2 and 3 and assess the potential impact. If you expect your income to be in the middle range (say, $35,000–$60,000), then don't let government payments influence your decision.

If that is your assumption, then my advice for the next five years is to concentrate on two things: maximizing your RRSP contributions and paying off all your debt. Don't go into retirement with a big debt-service cost hanging over your head. If you are not satisfied with your financial advisers, switch to someone who will work to help you achieve these goals.

RRSP Investments

SITTING IN CASH

Q I've parked 85 percent of my RRSP in cash in my self-directed RRSP. I'm 49 with six years to retirement, with a company pension of $3000 a month. Where should I invest this cash? I don't believe the market will take off any time soon.

A I cannot give you specific advice on where to put the money. You should consult with a financial adviser and set up a proper portfolio. But I can offer a few general thoughts.

By leaving your money in cash, you have protected your principal. However, the price you have paid for safety is a very low return. You could have done much better with, for example, short-term bond funds with almost no risk. Even GICs would have provided a better return.

With interest rates continuing low, you need to look at other options. Since you are nervous about the stock market, start exploring some alternatives. For example, you might consider setting up a portfolio that focuses on various types of income securities, such as bonds of varying maturities, preferred shares, GICs, REITs, and mortgage-backed securities. If you want to have some growth potential, add a few top-quality stocks, such as banks, utilities, and senior energy companies.

Your asset mix will be dictated by your risk/return balance. Since you appear to be very conservative and with retirement coming fast, you might consider a mix of 10 percent cash, 30 percent fixed-income securities (e.g., bonds, mortgages), 30 percent variable-income securities (e.g., REITs), and 30 percent blue-chip stocks. That's a decision to be made in consultation with your financial adviser.

WHERE TO INVEST?

Q I'm planning to invest $20,000 into my RRSP. I'm 51 years old and a medium risk taker. I would like to invest it for the next 7-to-10-year period. I was wondering if you can suggest what type of mutual fund product I can buy for this investment to get a better return. Also, I'm interested in ETF funds.

A Your best bet would be to choose a balanced fund with a history of above-average results. Given your age, a fund in the Canadian Neutral Balanced category would be appropriate. There are many from which to choose. One that I particularly like, and own myself, is Fidelity Monthly Income Fund, but I suggest you talk to a financial adviser before making a decision.

WANTS TO USE RRSP TO HOLD CONDO EQUITY

Q Can I use my RRSP funds to buy the equity in my condo? It is worth $117,000 and the mortgage is $77,000. Can I use my $40,000 in my RRSP to have my RRSP purchase the equity as a self-administered asset?

A No. An RRSP is not permitted to hold real estate directly, except in the very rare circumstance where the plan forecloses on a mortgage. Even then, the RRSP would have to sell the property within one year. RRSP mortgages are permitted, but you already have a substantial mortgage on the property. When the current term is up, you could convert it into an RRSP mortgage, but that is expensive.

NEEDS TO SELL A FUND

Q I need to cash in a mutual fund from my self-directed RRSP. Would you recommend one that is making money or one below its book value by 30 percent?

A The issue is not whether you should sell a winner or a loser. Rather, it's which fund is best suited for your long-term goals within the RRSP. Take a careful look at the two funds you are considering. Ask yourself which one fits better into your plans going forward from the point of view of asset mix, growth prospects, and risk. Make the decision on that basis.

RRSPs AND SMALL BUSINESSES

Q I would like to know if I could use my RRSP to purchase a business, and if so, would I be taxed on this amount?

A RRSP investments in the shares of small businesses are allowed as long as certain conditions are met. Limited partnership interests are also eligible. However, only qualifying small businesses are allowed. You should consult an accountant that specializes in this type of tax work to make sure your planned investment is onside.

WORRIED ABOUT RRSP STRATEGY

Q I am 31 years old and have been investing in my chartered-bank-held RRSP for eight years. I've put my money primarily (about 60 percent) in a balanced mutual fund, with additional investments in various other equity and sector funds. Despite having held the funds for all these years, the market value of my RRSP (about $15,000) is barely keeping up with the book value of the investment.

I had hoped, conservatively, for at least a 6 percent return, and understood that a diversified portfolio of mutual funds would compound in value over time. However, this has not been the case for my investments. I am concerned that although I am a long-term investor, when my retirement comes I will not have the nest egg I had planned for.

Currently, I intend to make about $5000 to $6000 in contributions per year going forward. I have just purchased my first home, a condominium, with a 25-percent down payment and intend to use any tax refund received to pay down the balance on the mortgage. In addition, I hold about $5000 in CSBs for an emergency fund and am debt free.

Should I be changing my investment strategy for my RRSP?

A Actually, to have come through the bear market without serious loss is a big accomplishment in its own right. So it would appear that your basic strategy is sound.

However, since you have 60 percent of your assets in a single fund, you need to look especially closely at how that specific fund is performing compared to its peer group. You have made it the pivot point for your whole plan, so if it is an underachiever, your RRSP will not perform to your expectations.

So some fine-tuning may be needed. The key is that balanced fund. If your RRSP is to be successful, you need a fund that outperforms the category average on a consistent basis.

WHAT ASSET MIX WILL GIVE THE RETURN
WE WANT?

Q We have a retirement plan that will achieve all our objectives. It is based on earning a 6 percent rate of return, over the long term. Should we build our portfolio according to the plan of a 6 percent rate of return? If so, what asset mix do you recommend for our portfolio?

A An average annual compound rate of return of 6 percent is a reasonable target over the long term. But to achieve it, you will have to accept a certain degree of risk.

Assuming you want a balanced portfolio and are using mutual funds/exchange-traded funds (ETFs), you will be looking at a mix of cash-type securities, fixed-income funds, and equity funds. If we assume an average annual return of

1.5 percent on the cash (remember we're talking long term here), 4 percent on the fixed-income funds, and 8 percent on the equity funds, we arrive at the following asset mix:

Cash-type securities: 5 percent

Income funds: 30 percent

Equity funds: 65 percent

If our target returns are met over time, the average annual growth in this portfolio would be about 6.5 percent.

INTERESTED IN F FUNDS

Q I am wondering if you have a list of Canadian mutual funds that offer F units. I have heard these recommended by others as having lower MERs because trailer fees are not paid to the dealers. Since I deal with a discount broker, I have not been provided with any investment advice and, hence, do not feel my returns should suffer because the broker is receiving trailer fees on my account. I am hoping to obtain a complete listing so I can research and choose a particular group to invest in.

A I do not know of any specific listing of F funds. However, you can check at GlobeInvestor, Morningstar Canada, or The Fund Library to see if a particular fund you are interested in offers F units.

Even if it does, you probably will not be able to acquire them through a discount broker. F shares are intended for fee-based accounts only. Those are accounts for which the adviser receives no commissions or trailer fees but instead collects an annual fee from the client based on total assets in the account. This fee is typically 1 percent to 1.5 percent.

If a broker sells F units into a non-fee-based account, he or she receives no compensation at all. Bay Street would soon be filled with panhandling ex-brokers!

Locked-In Plans

CAN'T GET AT RRSP MONEY

Q I have $55,000 in a locked-in RRSP. Recently, my husband went bankrupt in Quebec, and I had no choice but to do the same. I can't do anything with the money in the RRSP, and the bank doesn't want to take this for security for a loan. I'm a school-bus driver, so I work 10 months of the year. Is there anything I can do, like borrow from the RRSP, to pay off my car so then I can put back the money monthly? I'm sure you can help me on that.

A The bank won't take the RRSP as security for a loan because it is illegal to do so under Canadian tax law. So that's not an option.

Some provinces have introduced hardship provisions that allow people to make limited withdrawals from locked-in plans under specific conditions. You would need to check with the organization that administers pension plans in Quebec to see what their rules are in this regard.

The other option is to convert the RRSP to a LIF. That would enable you to begin making withdrawals from the plan, and you could use that money to pay the car loan. However, most provinces have an age restriction on the ability to do this (often not before age 55), so here again, check with the appropriate Quebec authority about the feasibility of this option.

WANTS TO USE LOCKED-IN PLAN FOR HOUSE

Q I have a pension that I would like to transfer to an RRSP. I understand that the RRSP must be locked in until my regular retirement date. My question is: Can I use that locked-in RRSP for a down payment on a house? (I am a first-time buyer).

A I assume that you are asking if a locked-in RRSP is eligible for the federal government's Home Buyers' Plan. The answer is no. Here is the relevant paragraph from the official Canada Revenue Agency guide: "Some RRSPs, such as locked-in or group RRSPs, do not allow you to withdraw funds from them. Your RRSP issuer can give you more information about the types of RRSPs that you have and whether or not withdrawals under the HBP can be made from them."

WANTS MONEY FROM PENSION PLAN

Q My husband has a pension plan, and we were wondering if we can take money out to pay off some debt and pay it back like an RRSP. We do not want to take out a lot, only some to ease our worries. We do not know if this could be done. Can you please advise?

A Lump-sum withdrawals from pension plans prior to retirement are not permitted. You can, however, make such withdrawals from locked-in RRSPs—the rules vary depending on the jurisdiction that administers the plan.

You cannot withdraw money from an RRSP of any type for the purpose you describe and then pay it back. The only permitted repayable withdrawals from RRSPs are for a first-time home purchase or to further your education under the Lifelong Learning Plan.

Sorry I can't give you better news.

FRUSTRATED BY LOCKED-IN PLAN

Q I have a self-directed locked-in retirement account (LIRA) with about $13,000 in it. I would like to deposit more money in it to bring the total above $15,000 (so I can avoid paying annual fees of $100). But the bank tells me that I am not allowed to deposit money in the account because it is locked in! I know that I can't withdraw money from a LIRA, but it makes no sense to me that it is also forbidden to deposit more money in it! Is the bank right about this?

A I'm afraid so. LIRAs are usually created as a result of the transfer of lump-sum pension credits into a personal account, and individuals are not permitted to make contributions to such locked-in plans. Nor would most people want to, because of the withdrawal restrictions that you mention.

If you have any other locked-in accounts, you could transfer them into this LIRA, which may get you over the

$15,000 level. Another option is to invest the money aggressively and hope that your returns will be enough to push you over the mark.

WHAT TO DO ABOUT PENSION?

Q I've been employed by the same company for 27 years. I am 46, and along with many other employees, I'll be losing my job shortly due to a merger. I have the choice of leaving my pension where it is or transferring it, but I'm at a loss as to what would be the best option.

Everyone has a different opinion. Most have concerns about what happens to the money if and when we die, and feel they should transfer it. You yourself had the opinion a while ago that it is best to leave it where it is if it's a defined benefit. Do you still have the same opinion?

A As a general rule, yes, I still have the same view about leaving the money in the pension plan. With a defined benefit pension, you know what you will be receiving. That is not the case if you put the money in a locked-in RRSP, which is the only alternative to the pension plan.

That said, you want to be sure that the pension plan is not seriously underfunded, as some are, and that the merged company is financially strong and will be in a position to continue making plan contributions in the future. So ask some hard questions of the plan administrator before you make a final decision.

In the event of death, you should ask the administrator what rules would apply. There should be a survivor's benefit of some kind. In the case of a locked-in RRSP, the assets would pass tax-free to your spouse/partner. If you don't have one, the total amount in the plan will be considered to have been taken into income in your final year and taxed accordingly.

NEEDS LIF MONEY

Q I am age 75, and I would like to get all my money out of my LIF. I have just under $20,000 left. Can I do this and what are the penalties? I am on a low income. I have only taken a low monthly stipend out.

A It used to be almost impossible to get money out of locked-in plans except through annual withdrawals. But in recent years, governments have eased the rules and made the conditions for withdrawal less onerous. The specifics vary depending on which jurisdiction has administrative responsibility for your plan. However, most provinces allow plans with small balances remaining to be collapsed. Check with the provincial organization that oversees pensions. If it is a federally regulated plan, it's under the jurisdiction of the Office of the Superintendent of Financial Institutions. Of course, tax will be assessed on the withdrawal.

BORROWING AGAINST A LIF

Q Is there any way you can borrow against your LIF with the loan being the LIF investment receiving the interest? Can the LIF purchase a bond or other security that can be used to secure an outside loan?

A The answer to both questions is no. RRIFs, LIFs, RRSPs, and LIRAs may not be used as loan collateral. However, Tax-Free Savings Accounts can.

Tax Issues

WORRIED ABOUT RRSP TAX

Q I hope you can help me. I have no income to claim for the 2013 year. I am 34. I am taking a fitness course and was approved for a student loan. I start college in January 2014, studying to be a child and youth care counsellor.

I want to cash in about $5000 of my RRSP investment just to pay my bills and give me a little money while I take the fitness course. Will I be penalized and have to pay lots in tax even though I will not have any income for the 2013 year? Any suggestions would be greatly appreciated.

A Yes, you will have to pay tax. And no, you won't. Let me explain the paradox.

Any RRSP withdrawals are subject to withholding tax. The financial institution has no discretion in this matter. On amounts up to $5000, the rate is 10 percent for all Canadians except Quebec residents. But here's a warning: If you go $1 over that level, the withholding tax jumps to 20 percent on the entire amount. So, to be safe, take out just under $5000.

The good news is that all that tax will be refunded when you file your 2013 return: Since you have no other income, your personal tax credit will more than cover the withdrawal.

WANTS TO AVOID TAXES ON CAPITAL GAINS

Q I have a question regarding stocks and self-administered RRSPs. I have set up a brokerage account with an initial investment of $10,000 in various stocks. Over the past year, I have made a $3600 profit on the initial $10,000. Now I want to set up an RRSP trading account to avoid the capital gain on my stock trading. I would like to know the tax implications of doing this over the course of, say, 20 to 30 years. Can I avoid the capital gains if the monies are left in the account until I retire? What would be the tax implications when I retire? Is there a better solution? Or should I stay with what I am doing now and claim the capital gains (or losses) on my income taxes?

A There is no way that you can avoid paying tax on the capital gains you have made in a non-registered account, unless you have capital losses to offset them against. If you transfer this account into a self-directed RRSP, that will be a "deemed disposition" as far as the CRA is concerned. That means that, for capital gains' purposes, you will be assumed to have sold the assets, and tax will become payable when you file your next return.

By the way, this does not apply with capital losses. You cannot transfer money-losing securities into an RRSP and claim a loss for doing so.

Looking into the future, keep in mind that any capital gains made within an RRSP will be taxed at your marginal rate when the money is finally withdrawn. You will not receive the 50-percent capital gains exemption that applies to your profits in the non-registered account.

CANADIANS GET THE SHORT END

Q I'm a Canadian working for a U.S.-based company. The Canadian employees in my office are questioning a company policy that gives all the U.S. employees a percentage of their salary, depending on the number of years of service, towards a retirement plan. This is over and above the amount that each individual contributes separately and that the company matches. Since this is a company policy, we've inquired as to why we do not get the same treatment if we work for the same company. We've been told that because of Canadian tax laws, they're unable to extend this benefit to us. Is this true? Do we have laws that don't allow a U.S.-based company to contribute to an RRSP on our behalf? Your help would be greatly appreciated as we've been fighting this issue for years.

A Your employers are correct when they say that Canadian tax laws do not allow anyone to contribute to an RRSP except the plan owner (or a spouse in the case of a spousal plan).

However, some companies with group RRSPs circumvent this rule by giving employees a wage increase equivalent to the amount that the firm would otherwise contribute to the plan, on condition that the money goes into the individual's RRSP. The extra income is taxable, but that is offset by the corresponding RRSP contribution, so the net tax impact on the employee is zero. The added salary is tax-deductible to the employer.

You don't make clear whether you are actually working in the U.S. or for a Canadian subsidiary of a U.S. company. In the latter case, the approach I've outlined would work for you and the other Canadian employees. However, if you are resident in the U.S. and pay taxes there, it's a different story, because U.S. tax laws will not allow you to claim a deduction for contributions to a Canadian RRSP. In that situation, you should consider opening a U.S. retirement account to which your employer can contribute.

UNDERSTANDING RESP RULES

Q If I put money into an RESP, can I personally draw it out? Does the child have to do this? Do you have to show receipts that it was used for educational purposes? I have an RRSP coming due, and would like to convert this to an RESP. I am a senior (65) and this would help a lot if I can avoid the income tax upon withdrawal in the future.

A Although RESPs (Registered Education Savings Plans) have been around for several years, there is still a lot of confusion about them. So let's deal with some of the issues raised here:

- *RESP capital withdrawals.* Capital invested in an RESP can be withdrawn by the donor at any time, tax-free. This is because no tax deduction is given for an RESP contribution (unlike RRSPs). You are investing with after-tax money, so you can have it back whenever you want.

- *RESP income withdrawals*. Income earned over the years on the invested capital is taxable when it is taken out of the plan. This money is paid out to the student and is taxed in his or her hands; it is not taxable to the donor. Since students usually have little income and enjoy extra tax credits, the tax payable should be negligible.
- *Receipts*. The government does not normally require receipts to prove that RESP money was used for educational purposes, but they should be kept available in the event of questions from the Canada Revenue Agency. The term "educational purposes" is very loosely defined, so almost any expense that has some educational relationship will pass muster.
- *RRSP conversion*. You cannot convert an RRSP to an RESP. There is no mechanism for doing this. The money would have to be withdrawn from the RRSP, which would make it taxable. Since RESP contributions are not tax-deductible, you cannot offset that tax cost in this way.

RRSP WITHDRAWALS AFFECTED CPP, OAS

Q My parents have approximately $100,000 in RRSPs. My father is 69 and has begun to make withdrawals. He quickly learned that any amount that is taken out of his RRSPs is deducted from his CPP/OAS. This arrangement penalizes people who have made the decision to save but have not saved enough to live comfortably without the aid of CPP/OAS. Is there any way that he can enjoy his savings without having funds deducted?

A What you say is technically not correct. RRSP withdrawals do not have any direct impact on the Canada Pension Plan and Old Age Security payments.

However, they may have the effect of moving your father into a higher tax bracket, which would mean that his after-tax return from the CPP/OAS is reduced. Also, if the RRSP withdrawals push his net income above $71,000, he will be subject to a special 15-percent "clawback" tax on his OAS payments. The CPP is not subject to any clawback tax.

WHAT TO DO WITH SEVERANCE?

Q I am getting a $23,000 severance package from work and have room in my RRSP to contribute to it. However, I need the money. Would it be better to roll it into the RRSP and then pull it out in small amounts if there is less tax this way? Or would it be better to take the cash, pay tax at 47 percent, and then purchase an RRSP and get the refund?

A Your strategy should be to pay as little tax as possible on your severance. Taking a 47-percent upfront hit does not make sense. If you do that, you will be left with only about $12,000 of the severance.

Arrange to have the money paid directly into the RRSP, which will tax-shelter the whole amount (assuming you have the contribution room). Then withdraw cash as needed. Presumably, you will be in a lower tax bracket next year, so the amount you get to keep after-tax should be significantly more. Plus any income earned inside the RRSP will grow in a tax-sheltered environment.

REGISTERED OR NON-REGISTERED?

Q I'm in my early 30s and have an RRSP and a non-registered account, the latter of which contains the bulk of my assets. I mostly invest in mutual funds. I've always considered that the benefit of a non-registered account is the freedom to invest anywhere, despite the tax disadvantage. How would you suggest a younger, more aggressive investor divide his or her money between registered and non-registered portfolios?

A There is no simple answer to your question. However, your description of yourself as an "aggressive" investor suggests that you are more interested in capital gains than in slow, steady growth over a long period. It also suggests that you are prepared to take more risks to achieve those profits.

In that case, the bulk of your mutual funds should continue to be held in your non-registered portfolio. The reason is simple: tax laws. Only 50 percent of your capital gains will be taxed, compared to the full amount if they are made within a registered plan (all RRSP/RRIF withdrawals are taxed at your marginal rate regardless of the original source of the income). As well, in a non-registered account, any capital losses that you sustain can be deducted from your capital gains. There is no relief for losses within an RRSP.

Of course, you are giving up the tax deduction you would

receive for your RRSP contributions if you take this course. So you'd better be sure that your investments generate enough gains to compensate for that.

Early Retirement

WHERE TO DRAW MONEY?

Q My husband and I are planning to retire within the next year—we're 53 and 45 years old. Our substantial retirement funds are split between a defined contribution pension plan, RRSPs, and savings.

Our analysis indicates that, post-retirement, we should draw down savings first followed by pension and RRSP. Can you please confirm this, or provide some guidance on what funds should be drawn when and why?

A First, may I say you are very fortunate to be able to retire so early. You must have a very skilled investment adviser (or be very talented in money management yourselves) for this to be possible. Many people have had to postpone their retirement dates because of losses suffered in the bear market of 2008–2009.

I assume that you have done a careful analysis and determined that you have adequate financial resources to support what is likely to be a very long period of retirement. One of the challenges to early retirement is the fact that the number of working years are reduced, while the number of years during which you must live off your capital is increased.

Now to your question. If you have to draw down capital

to live on, which you appear to be suggesting, then the first source should be your non-registered assets. This allows you to benefit from tax-sheltered investment growth within your pension plan and RRSPs for the maximum amount of time. That said, you should avoid depleting any capital for as long as possible, for the reasons I've already explained. Instead, try to construct an income program that combines cash flow from the pension plan with investment income from the non-registered account to provide the money you need.

RRSPs AFTER RETIREMENT

Q Are you allowed to put money into RRSPs when you are retired?

A There are two factors that determine your eligibility to contribute to an RRSP, and whether you are retired is not one of them. They are:

1. You must have earned income, or unused carry-forward room from earlier years. The definition of earned income specifically excludes money from pension plans, Canada Pension Plan, Old Age Security, and investments. However, net rental income is included, so if you own a revenue property, that can provide some RRSP room. Of course, any income you earn in retirement, perhaps from consulting or a part-time business, is also eligible.

2. You must be less than 72 years of age. You cannot have an RRSP after December 31 of the year in

which you turn 71. So you cannot make any RRSP contribution after that time—although you can make a final RRSP contribution during that year. However, if you have a younger spouse and earned income, you can contribute to his or her RRSP even if you are no longer entitled to have a plan yourself.

RRIF Conversion

CONVERT TO RRIF AT 53?

Q My wife (age 53) has stopped working and is not considering re-entering the workforce. She has a self-directed RRSP, and we are considering if it would be beneficial to convert this into a RRIF to allow her to receive a regular income. I have a good pension plan and intend to continue working for five or six more years.

A What's the point of converting to a RRIF now? There is nothing to stop your wife from making withdrawals from the RRSP whenever she wants, and in whatever amounts she requires. By converting to a RRIF, she would be faced with the requirement to make minimum annual withdrawals and could no longer contribute to the plan.

She may think now that she won't return to work, but she is still relatively young and may have a different view in a year or two. Retaining the RRSP keeps all the options open. She won't have to make withdrawals if she starts earning an income again, and she can resume contributions to the plan. In most cases, it doesn't make sense to convert an RRSP to a

RRIF before age 65, at which time you can convert enough
to claim a pension tax credit for the first $2000 withdrawn.

WHAT TO DO WITH THREE RRSPs?

Q I turn 69 at the end of this year and have RRSPs at three
different banks.

Should I consolidate all three to one bank or leave them
where they are and have three RRIF payments? Are there better
deals at one bank than at another? What should I look for?

A As a general rule, I advise people to consolidate all RRSPs
into a single RRIF. There are three reasons for this:

1. *Withdrawals.* You must make at least a minimum
   withdrawal from each RRIF you own. If you have
   several RRIFs, keeping track of the payments can
   become confusing. Better to have a single plan that
   issues payments when you require them (monthly,
   quarterly, annually).
2. *Cost.* Depending on the type of RRIF you have,
   there may be an annual administration fee involved.
   You'll pay this for each plan, regardless of how
   much money is in it.
3. *Ease of administration.* It's much simpler to monitor
   the assets of a single plan than it is to keep track of
   three different plans.

Regarding your question about which bank you should
deal with, there are no hard-and-fast rules. I suggest that you

speak to a representative at each of the banks where you now have an RRSP. Tell the person you intend to consolidate all your RRSPs into a single RRIF and ask what type of plan they will offer you. Specifically, request information on the fees they will charge, frequency of reports, interest rate paid on any guaranteed investment certificates you may have, investment counselling services, and flexibility to acquire other types of investments, such as mutual funds, which you may want to add to boost cash flow.

RRSPs AND MORTGAGE PAYMENTS

Q I have a small RRSP that I think I have to collapse in two years (at age 71). The amount is enough for a down payment on a condominium but not enough for the mortgage payments to be affordable. Can I invest the RRSP in debentures that will give me a bit of interest return without sacrificing anything, or everything, to the government in taxes?

A It's correct that you have to close the RRSP in the year you turn 71. However, you don't have to withdraw the money. You can convert to a RRIF or an annuity if you prefer.

If you take the money out of the RRSP as a lump sum to use for the down payment, it will become taxable and the government will take a large bite. As an alternative, see if you qualify for the Home Buyers' Plan. This will enable you to borrow the money interest-free from the RRSP for the down payment. There is no age limit for using the plan. At 71, you would proceed to convert the balance in the plan to a RRIF. Each year, instead of repaying the balance due on the

Home Buyers' Plan loan, simply declare it as income, which is permitted. The tax you pay will probably end up being much less than if you'd made a lump-sum withdrawal.

The remaining assets in the RRIF can be invested in debentures or anything else you wish. You will be required to make withdrawals from the RRIF, and this money can be used to help pay the monthly carrying cost of the condo. These payments are fully taxable.

HOW TO HANDLE TWO RRSPs

Q I have a considerable amount of money in two RRSP accounts, one being about $130,000 and the other well above that. Should I start using the smaller RRSP in order to take advantage of the pension reduction amount? If so, should I convert to a RRIF or turn it into an annuity?

A As a general rule, I prefer to wait until age 71 to convert RRSPs. This allows you to retain your planning flexibility for as long as possible. However, there are two reasons to consider converting at least some of your RRSP assets at age 65.

The first is to take advantage of the pension income amount. This allows you to claim up to $2000 and receive a 15-percent tax credit worth $300 off your federal tax payable. RRIF payments received from age 65 on qualify. However, if you are receiving $2000 or more from a workplace pension plan (not Canada Pension Plan or Old Age Security), then there is no point in converting any RRSP assets to a RRIF since you won't receive any additional credit.

The second reason to convert early is to take advantage of pension income splitting with your spouse. Lump-sum withdrawals from RRSPs are not eligible for income-splitting, but RRIF/LIF payments received from age 65 on do qualify. So if you expect to draw against your RRSP in the years between age 65 and age 71 and income splitting would be beneficial to you, converting at least some of the assets to a RRIF makes sense. This is a complex calculation so you may want to seek the advice of a tax planning professional before making a decision.

As for the annuity part of the question, I would definitely not recommend buying an annuity at age 65. The younger you are, the less monthly income you will receive, and that's especially true when interest rates are low.

MOVING ASSETS

Q What's the best way to transfer money from RRSPs to RRIFs?

A If possible, I suggest setting up a single RRIF and moving all of your RRSPs into it. You are legally allowed to have more than one RRIF, just as you can have multiple RRSPs. However, it is not a good idea. You have to make withdrawals from every RRIF you create and managing several sources of cash flow can be difficult. If you open a self-directed RRIF, you can arrange to have all your RRSPs transferred into it (all you'll have to do is sign the authorization documents). Once the plan is set up, you can make any changes to the portfolio you wish.

RRIF Strategies

USE RRIF TO PAY DEBT?

Q I have two lines of credit. I also have about $14,000 in RRIFs plus about $8000 in savings. Should I use this money to pay off one line of credit? It would make life easier since we are both seniors.

A Normally, I don't advise people to take money out of a registered plan to pay off debt, but this could be an exception. The amount in the RRIF is very small, so it is contributing very little to your income. Assuming you are in a low tax bracket, the tax penalty for withdrawing the whole amount and closing the plan should be minimal. Depending on your province of residence, your marginal tax rate on the withdrawal would probably be around 22 percent, which would leave you with about $11,000 to put towards the line of credit.

Whether you also want to deplete your savings account is another matter. It is always good to have some emergency cash. However, if you leave the line of credit open after paying it down, you could always draw against it in future should the need arise. In the meantime, you would not be paying interest.

COLLAPSING A RRIF

Q How long do I have to collapse a RRIF?

A Unlike RRSPs, there is no time limit on RRIFs. You can retain the plan for as long as you live. However, the government's minimum withdrawal percentage increases annually until it reaches a maximum of 20 percent of the plan's value at age 91. At that rate, the assets in the RRIF will diminish quickly so that by the time you reach 100 (thinking optimistically), there will be virtually nothing left. That's why I advise moving some funds into an annuity when you're in your eighties.

RRIF INVESTMENTS

Q I would like some suggestions as to the most appropriate investment for a RRIF.

A The two main objectives of a RRIF are to produce cash flow and protect capital. Therefore, the focus should be on low-risk, income-generating securities. When interest rates are high, monthly-pay GICs are a good choice, but when rates are low, I would not go that route. Here are some other possibilities:

- *Monthly income funds*. Many mutual funds offer regular monthly cash flow. However, they can be very different in terms of their investment mandate and portfolio composition. In order to minimize risk, avoid funds with a high equity component (60 percent or more). Funds in the Canadian Neutral Balanced and Canadian Fixed-Income Balanced categories will tend to be less volatile and therefore of lower risk.

- *Exchange-traded funds (ETFs)*. An increasing number of ETFs offer monthly distributions, and the carrying costs are much lower than for mutual funds. The iShares Diversified Monthly Income Fund is a good example. It trades on the Toronto Stock Exchange under the symbol XTR.
- *Bonds*. Even when interest rates are low, you can get decent returns from good-quality corporate bonds. Payments are usually made semi-annually. Ask your broker about possibilities. Alternatively, use a bond mutual fund or ETF.
- *Preferred shares*. These are much less risky than common stocks and pay regular dividends, usually quarterly or semi-annually. Fixed-rate preferreds always pay the same amount; floating-rate pre-ferreds have their rates tied to a benchmark such as the prime rate. Note that the payments will not be eligible for the dividend tax credit because they are received in a registered plan.
- *Dividend-paying stocks*. To reduce risk, focus on utilities, pipelines, telecoms, and banks. They won't be immune to a stock market collapse, but any losses should be limited. Just don't overload the RRIF with them.

25
Quiz Time

Now that you've come to the end, how much have you learned about RRSPs? To find out, take these two sets of quizzes. The first one deals with very basic issues, so you should score at least 80 percent on it. The second involves more complex matters, so 65 percent is a passing grade. If you fail the first test, you should read the book again. If you fail part two, go back to the relevant chapters and bring yourself up to speed. Ready? Here goes.

Test #1 – Basic Knowledge

1. What percentage of earned income are you allowed to contribute to an RRSP?
    a) 15
    b) 18
    c) 20
    d) 25

2. How long can you carry forward unused contribution room?
   a) Five years
   b) Seven years
   c) Ten years
   d) No time limit

3. How many days are you allowed after year-end to make an RRSP contribution and claim a deduction for the previous tax year?
   a) 30
   b) 45
   c) 60
   d) 90

4. How much can you borrow from your RRSP using the Home Buyers' Plan?
   a) $15,000
   b) $20,000
   c) $25,000
   d) $50,000

5. How many RRSPs can you have?
   a) One
   b) Two
   c) Five
   d) No limit

6. How much can you overcontribute to an RRSP without incurring a penalty?
   a) $2000
   b) $2500
   c) $3000
   d) No limit

7. How much can you withdraw from an RRSP tax-free?
   a) $1000
   b) $500
   c) Nothing
   d) No limit

8. You must claim an RRSP deduction for the year in which the contribution was made.
   a) True
   b) False

9. If you want to invest in the stock market, what type of RRSP do you need?
   a) A savings plan
   b) A mutual funds plan
   c) A self-directed plan
   d) None of the above—stocks aren't permitted in RRSPs

10. If you have the right kind of RRSP, you can contribute
    securities directly to it.
    a) True
    b) False

11. What interest rate is charged on an RRSP loan under the
    Lifelong Learning Plan?
    a) 1 percent
    b) 2 percent
    c) Prime rate
    d) Zero

12. How long do you have to repay loans under the Lifelong
    Learning Plan and the Home Buyers' Plan?
    a) 10 years
    b) 15 years
    c) 20 years
    d) 25 years

13. How long do you have to wait before withdrawing
    money from a spousal plan with no penalty?
    a) One year
    b) Three years
    c) Five years
    d) Zero years

14. It's impossible to get money from a locked-in RRSP unless it is converted to a LIF.
    a) True
    b) False

15. Which of the following is not a qualified RRSP investment?
    a) U.S. stocks
    b) Junk bonds
    c) Limited partnerships
    d) Real estate

ANSWERS

1. b	6. a	11. d
2. d	7. c	12. b
3. c	8. b	13. b
4. c	9. c	14. b
5. d	10. a	15. d

Test #2 – The Hard Stuff

1. Who was prime minister when the RRSP legislation was passed?
   a) John Diefenbaker
   b) Louis St. Laurent
   c) Lester Pearson
   d) Pierre Elliott Trudeau

2. Which of these mutual fund companies has the lowest management expense ratios (MERs)?
    a) Mackenzie Financial
    b) RBC
    c) Fidelity
    d) Steadyhand

3. What is Warren Buffett's first rule of investing?
    a) Never invest in things you don't understand.
    b) Buy low, sell high.
    c) Avoid airline stocks.
    d) Don't lose money.

4. How often should you review your RRSP investments?
    a) Annually
    b) Semi-annually
    c) Quarterly
    d) Monthly

5. Which of the following is *not* considered to be a cash-type investment?
    a) Treasury bills
    b) Bonds
    c) Money market funds
    d) Bankers' acceptances

6. Dividends paid to an RRSP from U.S. companies are not subject to the usual cross-border withholding tax. How much is that tax?
   a) 5 percent
   b) 10 percent
   c) 15 percent
   d) 25 percent

7. What percentage of the RRSP of a person between ages 26 and 50 should be allocated to growth securities?
   a) 45–60 percent
   b) 50–70 percent
   c) 40–55 percent
   d) 30–40 percent

8. When is a TFSA a better choice than an RRSP?
   a) If you expect your income in retirement to be higher than it is now.
   b) If you expect to apply for the Guaranteed Income Supplement when you retire.
   c) If you have a gilt-edged defined benefit pension plan.
   d) All of the above.

9. Which of the following is not eligible for the Home Buyers' Plan?
    a) A condo
    b) A summer cottage
    c) A mobile home
    d) A resale home

10. What limits does the government place on the use of money borrowed under the Lifelong Learning Plan?
    a) The money can only be spent on tuition fees.
    b) The money must be used for "educational purposes."
    c) The money can only be used to attend Canadian schools.
    d) There are no limitations.

11. Which of the following reasons can be used to access money in locked-in plans administered by the federal government?
    a) Financial hardship
    b) Shortened life expectancy
    c) Leaving Canada for at least two years
    d) All of the above

12. Which agency is responsible for overseeing locked-in RRSPs in British Columbia?
    a) Office of the Superintendent of Financial Institutions
    b) Financial Services Commission
    c) British Columbia Pension Board
    d) Financial Institutions Commission

13. What percentage is withheld for tax purposes on RRSP withdrawals of more than $15,000 in all provinces except Quebec?
    a) 10 percent
    b) 15 percent
    c) 25 percent
    d) 30 percent

14. Which of the following is legally permitted under certain conditions?
    a) Transferring RRSP assets to a TFSA.
    b) Transferring RESP assets to an RRSP.
    c) Transferring your RRSP assets to the RRSP of an adult child.
    d) None of the above.

15. How much will an annual RRSP contribution of $1200 be worth after 40 years at an average yearly growth rate of 6 percent?
    a) $141,745
    b) $196,857
    c) $335,737
    d) $418,726

ANSWERS

1. b	6. c	11. d
2. d	7. b	12. d
3. d	8. d	13. d
4. c	9. b	14. b
5. b	10. d	15. b

For More Investment Information

Tax-Free Savings Accounts

Tax-Free Savings Accounts are the most powerful investment option for Canadians since the introduction of RRSPs more than half a century ago. They offer an opportunity for even modest-income people to amass a small fortune over time—and perhaps even attain millionaire status. But they have to be managed properly.

Unfortunately, many people still don't know how to do that. They keep their money in savings accounts or GICs that pay almost nothing. They make mistakes with their withdrawals and get into trouble with the tax department as a result. They don't make the effort to understand the fees and get hit with unexpected charges. In short, they're squandering a chance at a million.

Gordon Pape wrote the first book on TFSAs ever published in Canada, and it became a huge bestseller. He followed that with *The Ultimate TFSA Guide*, which has been used successfully by many Canadians seeking to improve their returns.

This revised and updated edition includes details of rule changes, suggested investment strategies, dangers to watch for, and more. Key points:

- How to choose the right plan
- Questions to ask when opening an account
- Recommended TFSA investments
- Model portfolios
- Ways to maximize tax savings
- TFSA or RRSP?
- Using a TFSA to get a loan
- Passing assets to heirs
- Readers' questions answered

Retirement's Harsh New Realities

In this hard-hitting book, Gordon Pape pulls no punches in explaining the realities of retirement that confront Canadians, including collapsing pension plans, government inertia, a tax system that works against older people, pitiful savings rates, and the fact that there are no safe investments. And this is just the beginning, he writes. We are about to experience a series of wrenching changes in our retirement system as governments, corporations, and individuals struggle to cope with a tidal wave of harsh economic, demographic, and social realities.

But, as he puts it, "there are solutions to all problems," and this book offers them. Pape shares his common sense advice to help readers understand the realities of retirement and offers sound, practical solutions for protecting your family's future in a rapidly changing world. Inside you'll find advice on:

- Why a demographic crisis is creating widespread social unrest
- The Baby Boomer retirement crunch and what it means
- The failing pension system and what to do about it
- How to benefit from RRSPs and TFSAs
- Tips for reducing the tax hit
- How to succeed in today's turbulent investment climate
- Avoiding the crisis: how to protect your future

Despite the harsh new realities, Pape provides workable solutions to every problem. If it's not already, retirement planning must become one of your life's priorities.

Money Savvy Kids

Most of us grew up knowing very little about money and how to manage it. The result is the most indebted generation in Canadian history. Don't let your children make the same mistakes. This fun-to-read book by Gordon Pape and his daughter, Deborah Kerbel, will help get them, and you, on the right track. It contains sound practical information from Canada's most trusted financial writer, plus many delightful and sometimes hilarious personal anecdotes and children's quotes that will leave you laughing while you learn. Some highlights:

- How to teach the "value" of money
- Are allowances a good idea, and if so, how much?
- Saving, spending, and sharing
- Teaching your kids to shop smart
- Coping with children-directed advertising
- Games that teach money skills
- Great websites and apps—some reviewed by the kids themselves
- Money-smart books for young readers
- Saving for college

This book is a must-read for all parents with children between the ages of 5 and 17. Don't miss it.

Newsletters

Gordon Pape is the editor and publisher of these investment newsletters.

Internet Wealth Builder. This weekly email newsletter covers all aspects of investing and money management, including stocks, bonds, mutual funds, income trusts, taxes, and general economic comment. The seasoned team of contributing editors includes some of Canada's best investment minds. The newsletter takes a conservative approach to money management and was among the first to warn of the drop in the Toronto Stock Exchange in a lead article published in mid-June 2008, just a few days after the

TSX hit an all-time high. Since then, it has recommended many securities that have earned large profits for its readers.

The Income Investor. This twice-monthly newsletter focuses on income-generating securities with the goal of providing readers with above-average returns consistent with reasonable risk. At a time when interest rates are low and income trusts have been virtually phased out of existence, the guidance provided by this letter is vital to anyone seeking steady cash flow from their investments.

For information on these newsletters, visit www.Building Wealth.ca or call toll-free 1-888-287-8229.

Website

More financial information from Gordon Pape can be found at www.BuildingWealth.ca. The site offers free investment articles, a Q&A feature, book excerpts, and more information on his newsletters.

Acknowledgments

The information in this book has been gathered over many years, with the assistance of a number of people in both the public and private sectors. I would like to thank them collectively for their time and patience in helping me to understand some of the more complex areas of tax law to the extent that I have been able to explain them here in terms we can all understand.

I would especially like to thank the team at Penguin Canada, led by my long-time editor, Andrea Magyar, for their encouragement and support over the years. Special thanks to my production editor, Sandra Tooze, and my copy editor, Eleanor Gasparik.

Also, I want to thank my chief researcher (and daughter), Kim Pape-Green, who also prepared the index for this and many of my other books.

A writer may appear to work alone, but in fact it takes a professional team to make a book a reality and get it into the hands of those who want to read it. The team that has worked with me is one of the best in Canada. Thank you all.

Index